Girls With Dreams

Natasha Ravinand

To my mother, father, and sister
who never cease to make me laugh.

CONTENTS

ACKNOWLEDGMENTS

Many thanks to Tiffany and David Pham of Mogul Inc., whose input on gender inequality in the tech workplace was indispensable, Sara Mauskopf, Diane Barram Westgate, Shenaz Zack Mistry, Vanessa Ganaden, and Isabelle Zhou for their candid accounts of being women in tech, William Taormina and Greg Kaplan for their guidance and perspective, and my teachers Marina Alburger and Angie Olivares for their support and advice.

PAST, PRESENT, AND FUTURE

It's the 1930s.

Within the sprawling campus of Yale University, a young woman works away in a classroom. Scribbling equations and numbers, her every movement on the page is swift and deliberate. The pen obeys her every command. The ink presses onto the pages, searing its own distinct mark. Her eyes follow every line, and the lines follow every number, strung together, in a series of digits with enigmatic meanings and possibilities. It's 1934: less than twenty years since women around the country secured the right to vote and hold elected office. Her field consists of male engineers, mathematicians, scientists, and researchers. She is relatively alone, but there she is – still scribbling away at those numbers. With every written digit, she climbs closer and closer to finishing her work. Amazing Grace Hopper was bound to change the world.

Just after Hopper earns her Ph.D. from Yale in mathematics, World War II ignites. America is locked in a pivotal battle against the Axis powers, and against the might of the Pacific front. Cutting-edge technology is needed now, more than ever, and Hopper is eager to serve her country. Already an assistant professor at Vassar College, she chooses to work as a research fellow at Harvard University on a Navy contract. Her job? Working on the advanced Mark I computer.

Unlike today's machines, the Mark I was a massive device, held together by hundreds of miles of wire, a plethora of switches, and dozens of electromechanical components. A general purpose instrument, the Mark I is quintessential to the war effort, later being used by the Manhattan Project to defeat Japan. But even after the conflict had ended in victory, Hopper intended to continue on her studies and change the face of code as we know it.

Hopper seemed to ask herself why couldn't anyone, just anyone, learn how to code? And more importantly, why should we limit ourselves to outdated machine-speak when we can be developing better things faster and easier? So she has a sort of lightbulb moment, and she asks, what can I do to push the limits of computerization? And brilliantly, she dreams the idea of a compiler.

Now, when you program a computer program today, you type in code (whether it be in Java, Python, C++, or any other language) and you run it through a compiler. This compiler takes the code you have written and acts as a translator. For example, if I only know English, and I travel to Japan, I have a distinct language barrier with many of the people there. As a result, my abilities to complete a task are greatly undermined. However, if I have a translator that could translate my English into Japanese, and Japanese back to English, whatever I say and hear would be understood. Similarly, when we look to compilers, we are allowed to have a sort of middle ground where both sides can understand each other. This mutual sharing of knowledge is what allows so many people to start coding immediately. One of the most simple commands in the Python language is the print command. It does exactly what it sounds like – it prints a word onto your screen! And what do you need to type? To say hello, all you need to type is:

```
print("Hello")
```

Google an online Python compiler and give it a try!

But in Hopper's time, it was not nearly as easy. Computers were programmed in archaic machine-level code. Even in today's devices, all computers are powered by something called binary code. Coming from the Latin root (binary meaning two), the idea of two forms is essential when understanding how this cipher works. In a computer, every single action is controlled by binary code, and this code only has two digits: 1 and 0! That's right — every action a computer processes or carries out is dictated by a simple combination of 1s and 0s.

Similarly, instead of typing English words, scientists spent years learning the intricacies of manual programming and machine-level code. For example, when one wanted to type a command to a computer, it would appear as a random selection of letters and numbers strung together. It made no sense, and was definitely not as easy to understand as Python is today. As a result, not many were able to acquire the skill of programming, and few were able to learn it incredibly well.

Hopper decided that she would attempt to change the face of computing by creating a compiler. This was unheard of, revolutionary, and had never been done before. Moreover, countless of her peers, colleagues, and friends advised her that computers solely existed for arithmetic, and that programming had its limits in everyday usages. Don't fix something that isn't broken, they said. Computers can't understand English, they pressured. But that didn't stop Grace, because she had a dream: and she had every intention of making it reality.

And as it turns out, in 1952, Hopper produces a fully working compiler, translating mathematical notation into actual machine code. She names it the A compiler, with its first version being A-0. She has done the impossible — and it's groundbreaking. She has now pioneered the field of high-level language: specifically, using English words in programming commands. Hopper expressed that "[that] was the beginning of COBOL, a computer language for data processors. I could say, 'Subtract income tax from pay' instead of trying to write that in octal code or using all kinds of symbols." In later years, Hopper would aid the United States government by implementing principles of COBOL and FORTRAN (used in scientific programming) by testing and examining computer components. Hopper would later develop and implement more software for the Navy and was promoted to the rank of rear admiral by her retirement. At the time, she belonged to a small group of female admirals in the organization.

Hopper goes on the win the Man of the Year award in 1969 from the Data Processing Management Association. It's an ironic win, but well-deserved given the plethora of contributions she had bestowed upon the world of code. After her death in 1992, she is mourned by many and is posthumously given the Presidential Medal of Freedom in 2016 by President Barack Obama. Thousands upon thousands in the world of tech owe many of their discoveries to her, from artificial intelligence to app design. From Snapchat to cybersecurity — users and developers of anything tech related can thank Hopper. Even Anita Borg, a notable female computer scientist, designated the official annual women's event in computing to be the Grace Hopper Celebration.

Although she's regarded as the Queen of Code now, Hopper faced large, systemic discrimination when alive. After all, she lived in a tumultuous America with its Jim Crow segregation and widely misogynistic culture. Winning the right to vote in 1920, women were just starting to climb up the socioeconomic ladder during her studies in the '30s. Traditional gender norms permeated all facets of life, and it was much more normal for a woman to lead her life as a homemaker and caretaker than pursue graduate studies in mathematics and science. Women choosing to earn degrees in engineering and applying them were virtually unheard of in a time where the chief duty of a woman was to maintain the household. But Hopper was neither normal nor ordinary. A visionary and pioneer, she broke these barriers for herself and the women around her, contributing to American society in lasting ways. Without her, coding would still be an archaic process inaccessible to many, and we might not have built the incredible applications and devices we see now.

Today, with a Wi-Fi connection and a laptop, anyone can learn to program — yes, even you! I've learned many of my skills from websites all over the internet, and the reputable ones are very reliable and expertly taught. I like to believe that software development, and nearly all types of coding, are the perfect intersection between the arts and the sciences, as you need both to create a successful model or prototype. But contrary to popular belief, coding isn't just limited to hacking or cyber security — you can create games, build robots, and even animate with coding! Modern organizations such as Codecademy, Udacity, and Khan Academy pride themselves on being able to teach others how to program on a global scale. But none of these websites could exist if Hopper had not taken the first step to create the world's first compiler.

As to be expected, Hopper's journey was not without obstacles; namely, a lack of like-minded female peers. But what are we saying to the young Grace Hopper of today who is pressured away from STEM (Science, Technology, Engineering and Math) due to gender discrimination?

When I was younger, I used to constantly watch television. Every day, after waging a tiring crusade in my third grade classes, I would run home to unwind and relax with a bowl of trail mix and pancakes. As it happened, I was mildly obsessed with a show called *The Adventures of Jimmy Neutron: Boy Genius*. Premiering in 2002, it centered around a young, suburban boy named Jimmy, living with his parents Hugh and Judy Neutron in the town of Retroville. Jimmy, along with his friends Carl and Sheen, traveled the city in search of adventure after adventure. He was, in fact, a literal boy genius. Complete with his own secret lab, he would use the power of science to save the day from whatever chaos ensued and would receive steady applause from Retroville's citizens. The trio in itself was dork-like, and as a result, they would often have trouble conversing with female peers Cindy and Libby.

The girls were hardly mathematical prodigies. Libby was obsessed with her clothes, constantly stylish, and never untruthful. She would flaunt the newest fashion, perform average at school, and blindly follow whatever plot Jimmy had concocted. Cindy, on the other hand, longingly pined after him. Every episode, especially as they grew older, featured Cindy running longingly beside Jimmy, wishing that they could be together — with Jimmy reciprocating minimally. Although she seemed smart, her priorities were centered around him and not around 'saving the day' or being a leader. She was more than capable, however, and the writers made this clear; Cindy Vortex was a smart girl. But her plot line would exclusively develop around Jimmy's, and where Cindy could have had meaningful input, she was reserved to be placed in the same typecast so many fictional women are directed to: the love interest of a particular someone. She never had a chance to further her unique voice, and was left in the shadows of the male protagonist.

But what do the writers of a 2000's children's TV show have to do with Grace Hopper, or girls interested in technology?

Our world has made tremendous progress within a variety of matters. However, there is always more road to travel, and in the area of girls in STEM (Science, Technology, Engineering and Math), there is still much work to be done. Equality has not been reached — not in numbers or bias. Grace Hopper broke the barriers of women shaping the world through technology, but it is the subtlety in examples like *Jimmy Neutron* that continues building the wall. The significance of this is clear: the problem with the gender gap in STEM is one that can be directly traced to society. The dangerous property is its quiet bias — something that is never apparent in our minds but forever permeates it.

So in order to fully understand this problem, it is necessary to know the context. At this moment, there is a severe shortage of qualified females in STEM (specifically computer science). As the years go by, and progress is seemingly attained, the matter rages on, quietly in the background. What is ironic, however, is how the tech field is perceived as furthering society and progressing the future. But when we still hold age-old, traditional views and biases, these advancements can never truly be attained. And as this issue is two-pronged, we must first delve into the inequality by way of numbers.

In 2017, tech giant Microsoft commissioned a survey composed of a selection of girls in Europe. They were looking to find any patterns between age and scientific interest. If there is a shortage of girls in science, might they just not be interested in it? Although that seems like a logical hypothesis, it is far from the truth. In reality, what Microsoft found was that girls in Europe become incredibly interested in STEM at around age 11. They might explore various STEM-related activities, like their local science fair or LEGO robotics competition. But, this fascination soon plummets as they enter the brunt of their teenage years. Even more surprisingly, 6 out of every 10 girls disclosed that they would be more confident in pursuing STEM if it were equally populated with men and women.

The U.S. Department of Commerce noted in their specialist report *Women in STEM: A Gender Gap to Innovation* that women hold nearly half of all jobs in the United States. This includes any occupation, from agricultural, to service, creative, and even technology. However, the report showed that, when it came to the number of women in any career related to computer science, the percentage was just 24 to 29%. This demonstrates beyond doubt that the tech gender divide is not a consequence of a lack of females in the workplace. In fact, some occupations have a higher percentage of women than men (like the hospitality field, for example). So it is quite strange to see such a disparity in gender when examining the tech field. And this happens to be further concentrated in certain areas in STEM. In engineering, the percentages are even farther apart, with only 14% of all engineers being women in 2009. Within the applied sciences, this divide is even larger! And although the tech sector might pride itself in progressing society for the future, it isn't progressing female employees' checkbooks — at least, not nearly as much as those of their male counterparts. There is still a 14% wage gap, with women being paid, on average, $0.86 for every $1.00 a man makes. Although grounded skeptics might argue that the wage gap is a myth, don't buy into it: they're not the ones looking at the overall facts, or the whole story.

And it doesn't stop there. The problem isn't just concentrated around the middle ground, because it permeates the uppermost levels as well. The American Equal Employment Opportunity Commission stated within their *Diversity in Tech* report (May 2016) that 80% of all the top executives in U.S. technology are men, with only 20% identifying as women. And the same is true for virtually any sizeable industry.

For example, let's say we ventured into a conference for a top tech company. We walk in through the gleaming doors, head across the lobby, and enter the elevators. We're on our way to meet the board of the organization, and we couldn't be more excited. When we get to the uppermost floor, we make our way across the hall, and into the office section. We walk into the conference room, and we're met with an all-male executive board. That doesn't seem that strange to us, right? But let's say, in turn, we walk in and it is an all-female board. Wait, what? Suddenly that doesn't look quite right. Nowhere on the website did it say the company had some special mission in serving females. This is just a standard tech company centered around consumable media, like Twitter or Snapchat. So why is it composed of all females?

See, many don't have that type of reaction when met with males, as we're conditioned to think this way. And if you did, you're not a bad person — even as an avid feminist, I still find myself in these situations. But because of this mentality, many promising women are not obtaining the same chance as their male counterparts to lead and shape companies. This is absolutely critical, because if women aren't acquiring leadership roles, we cannot promote equality across the board. How can we change the entire establishment if we aren't taking care of the problem from the top-down?

But as a teenage girl passionate about computer science, this is evident. It's ingrained within us from childhood to see these fields being 'for guys', and this idea has existed for so long that we regard it as fact. It's traditional thinking that 'boys are good at math' and 'girls are good at reading', but the fact is, anyone can be good at anything if they put their minds to it. The unfortunate part is that this bias couldn't be further from any truth, and although previous generations have broken down barriers, they have not broken down the wall. It isn't simply black and white — because this isn't just a gender problem. This is a racial problem as well, and it has rooted itself deep within our society. So let's take a look into some more numbers to really try to get to the cause of the problem.

The U.S. Census Bureau, a data-collecting federal agency, released a report titled *Disparities in STEM Employment by Sex, Race, and Hispanic Origin* in September of 2013. Within it were some alarming realizations. For example, Caucasians and Asians absolutely dominate computer science and STEM fields. Caucasians make up a large 70.8% of the total STEM workforce, and with Asians making up 14.5%. Taking into account the low amount of Asians in the populace versus Caucasians, there is obvious, disproportionate representation here. When Asians are such a small part of the U.S. population overall, why are so many of them concentrated in STEM, and so many African-Americans and Hispanics noticeably absent? After all, where is everyone else? America is the land of immigrants, the land of people from all walks of life — but where is everyone?

Well, they're here. People of Hispanic and African-American ascent have lived in the U.S. across the centuries, working in various fields and making due progress. But the question that should be on everyone's mind is where are they in STEM?

They're present, but at much smaller rates than Asians and Caucasians. Hispanics make up 6.5% of the tech sector, with African-Americans close behind at 6.4%. Native Americans barely pull in at 0.4%. However, when you consider the fact that these races combined populate much more of the nation than Asian-Americans, a lack of representation becomes very clear. This is where you begin to enter the realm of societal bias, because it's not just in entry-level positions, or middle-level management. As with gender disparities, it's present at the top, and that is perhaps the most disconcerting thing.

The Equal Employment Opportunity Commission restated again in their report (*Diversity in Tech*) that Caucasians are the supreme majority when it comes to assuming tech executive positions, making up an astonishing 83.3% across the board. In fact, Caucasian men are unconditionally the norm, with very few women climbing up the ladder. Among a plethora of executives at the STEM-based Silicon Valley, only 1.6% were Hispanic, and 1% African-American. The amount of Native Americans present was close to none.

There is an obvious lack of diversity occurring in STEM. The good news is, though, that there are girls like you and me out there who are willing to break the stereotype, willing to break the barriers, and more importantly, willing to break the wall — the wall that has stood for years and years, and will undoubtedly crumble if we work together and find a solution. This stereotype is directly inhibiting girls like us from pursuing their dreams and making progress in the world of tech. But, it can get difficult when you consider all the obstacles ahead of us and all the road that is needing to be paved first. Personally, I'm well aware of this inequality and I've experienced it myself too. I followed a very similar path that many girls in developed countries go through. You see, at the age of eight, I became a scientist.

The Christmas of 2009 was a memorable one. Lights, presents, and festive candles decorated the joyful venue that was my home. Family members gathered to share stories and make witty banter, with dessert wine gently spreading its aroma minute by minute across the kitchen. I had just turned eight, with my birthday only a few months before. As per the family tradition, presents were due, and to my mild dismay, I was to wait with the rest of my cousins till the early evening to open them.

However, once the hour of five o'clock turned, I unwrapped my gift in quick haste and was immediately disappointed. I had begged for a scooter, or perhaps a softball mitt, but nothing even remotely of this nature laid in the box before me.

Instead, I found myself gazing at an educational, informative, quote-in-quote "Thames and Kosmos Physics Pro V1 Science Kit", decorated with a popping velvet ribbon and a faded Walmart sticker. It wasn't surprising; with my father being an engineer and my mother an avid pursuer of the sciences, it was only to be expected. While they stood grinning, complete with their Nikon cameras, I sat meekly near the pine tree. The problem was, I hated science. 3rd grade ecology was difficult enough to understand, and big words like 'gravitational force' and 'electronegativity' had too many letters for me to pay the slightest attention to. I was hardly the best in my class, by any token. I opted for other classmates to answer questions and, for the most part, avoided contributing much.

Manners held me in check as I hugged my parents and gleefully cheered that it was always what I had wanted, and that I was surprised they'd gotten it, for the first time, right. However, a part of me could not help thinking that a gift like this, as I academically put it to my friends at school, was 'lame'. But one day, I finally decided to open my "Thames and Kosmos Physics Pro V1 Science Kit" that was expertly hidden under my bed. Out of sight, and out of mind.

I absolutely loved it.

It was not merely a toy — it taught me basic physics and motors by having me apply myself to something productive. With it, I learnt to assemble tiny motors and gears, and even created a small fan. I used their parts to build a horn that would blare whenever the corresponding button was triggered, and came close to putting together a very small and simple game. Afternoons and evenings were spent on my plaid patched bed, with its blue and green threading, sprawled all over, hovering over this modest kit. I was now nine, and the possibilities seemed endless to me in a uniquely youthful way.

I found myself with an even greater curiosity than before. Initially, I was interested to know what things are, but what I wanted to know now was why and how they worked. At school, my interests in the sciences only advanced. I continually asked questions in my classes, was promoted to the gifted program, and enjoyed working with my peers to pen solutions and answers to the problems we encountered. I strived to excel, exerting a confidence that I had never felt before. I became a leader, and believed in what I could accomplish. I was proud of my progress and what I was trying to achieve.

I showed similar appreciations in mathematics. A difficult subject for me, I had always struggled with feelings of inadequacy. However, I now tried to reason out with the problems instead of resorting to ceaseless frustration. Attaining the patience to learn was the opening of new gates for me. It continued well like this for some years.

Everything changed when I became a teenager. Like clockwork, it all started the fall I became thirteen.

I began the eighth grade at a different school, hundreds of miles from my familiar, previous junior high. I felt alone, friendless, and without a plan. Eventually, I found people with similar interests and paths as me, and life began to slowly move normally. A move, regardless of age, is always difficult. However, several other things were happening at the same time.

I experienced a decrease in my perception of personal aptitude — I no longer felt sure in myself. Many of my female peers felt the same. Part of that was comforting; to know that what you are feeling is common makes it seem mundane but also thankfully normal. The thing that perplexed me was this: why could I not view the same symptoms in the boys?

Symptoms being a lack of confidence, being a follower rather than a leader, and not speaking up when you disagreed with what was being said. The boys only seemed to become more confident, and in our math and science classes, especially so. I was not able to comprehend it, nor did I try too hard to. I thought that that's probably just the way it is.

I accepted it as fact and would not be able to see why that was so till a few years later when I was well into high school. Only then would I realize that societal constructs and expectations had taken me from a confident and progressing girl to a young person unsure of herself — even where she was more than capable.

Perhaps the most affecting part of this phase is what gradually took place in my scientific interests. Naturally, I began joining organizations that specialized in robotics and coding, as these activities interested me. I was ecstatic to find out that my high school had introduced a computer science club, and I was excited to confer with like-minded people. However, I soon observed that although the organization at my school had members upon members, I could not witness a single girl among the masses. Instead, groups of bros would huddle together to talk about code, throwing around irrelevant jargon, each trying to prove that they were smarter than the next guy.

I then tried to enter robotics, in hopes the gender ratio would be a bit more balanced, but to no avail. I witnessed the same type of 'bro culture' of boys exclusively hanging out together. I then soon quit robotics as my ideas were never valued and even cast aside by my male teammates. I had no input on the creative or mechanical process, because it was assumed — and I was even told — that I had "no idea what I was talking about". I was left out of meetings, not included in the build, and rarely acknowledged as a team member. I had, in fact, read entire manuals and researched thoroughly. The credit for most of my work was taken not by me but by my louder and more aggressive teammates, who spoke above me. Even the coach subtly disregarded my feedback in favor of my male peers — and frequently as well. I ignored it, citing that I was probably over-analyzing the situation.

As I grew older, I started hearing certain phrases here and there, out and about, everywhere and anywhere. When I expressed my career interests in engineering, I would hear, "Isn't that a bit difficult for someone like you?". They would subconsciously direct me to English, other liberal arts, and sometimes even childcare. A family friend once talked to my father separately to make sure I was indeed "on the right path".

What frustrated me was that this was an initial reaction; no advanced thought had been placed beyond it other than the fact that I was female. Family members have intentionally dumbed down professional jargon in talks with me because they assume I am not capable of understanding. However, when talking with an even younger male relative, they choose their words much less carefully. A teacher once asked me if I really wanted to do my career report on engineering — just to make sure. After all, most of the other girls were doing actresses, models, and fashion stars. She didn't want me to regret my decision, as I couldn't change it.

At first, my reactions to all of these incidents, and ones of the like, were of anger. I kept thinking, why should my gender be any more important than my favorite color, hairstyle, or music preferences? If anything, I believed that my actual aptitude for coding or creativity should be the primary factor in any judgments. If we don't judge people on whether they like apples or not, why should we judge their gender?

However, after years of subconscious and conscious conditioning, that anger soon subsided to insecurity and a sense of uncertainty. I was now not the slightest bit confident in any of my preconceived skills. I felt intimidation from my male peers, intended or not. STEM organizations were not inclusive, as I had no peers — the only ones there were groups of boys who were 'bros', crowded over one another, closed off like a wall.

It reached me in other ways as well. For example, whenever someone asked me about my coding experience, I habitually replied that it was minimal and I was not capable of actually developing something. Whenever I talked to a male peer about technology, I was afraid to speak my mind out of fear of condescension. Experiencing this over a prolonged period changed something within myself. I missed the confidence I had.

But, when I entered my freshman year in high school, some things began to make sense. I started getting involved with many organizations on campus dedicated to the feminist cause, including the National Organization of Women and Girls Who Code. Meeting like-minded females and males created a positive atmosphere for me to safely explore why I felt the way I had.

I soon began to realize that it was all about my and millions of other girls' struggle to fit within society's expectations and constructs. Girls typically are not expected to progress within the maths and sciences, leading to an influx of females pursuing the arts, and a select few forfeiting their passion for science to avoid harassment. Yes — actual harassment. This is only further hurt by the growing bro culture within tech — an environment comfortable for men and only men.

Pioneers like Margaret Hamilton, Rosalind Franklin, and Grace Hopper had not been recognized enough till now for their extraordinary achievements. If you're the average American, you probably have never heard of them. As a result, we as a society must foster a safe and fulfilling environment to be valued, whether it be in the arts, maths, or sciences.

At this point in time, we're in danger of turning away the next Grace Hopper, and we must do everything in our power to make sure that doesn't happen. We need to keep learning, keep progressing, and most importantly, keep breaking those barriers down.

And perhaps we might be the first to break the wall.

THE CHALLENGE AHEAD

A Los Angeles Target.

Summer of 2010.

The children's section.

Being nine years old, I was ecstatic when my father allowed me to shop for my own birthday present. I had never been entrusted with as much responsibility as this, so I treated the opportunity with great reverence. I ran to the toy section, a multitude of possibilities flying over me. Being an avid fan of *Star Wars*, I had seen all the movies, all of the TV shows, and owned multiple items of merchandise. My father had purchased a replica lightsaber, which lit up with LED lights and had installed sound devices to imitate the props used in the movies. It glowed a bright blue and was a treasured item throughout my childhood.

It was only natural for me to choose a Star Wars toy, as anything else was considered blasphemy in the strongest sense. I carefully made my way to the Star Wars section, and a beautiful sight caught my eye: an exact replica of a Stormtrooper blaster as shown in *Attack of the Clones*. My hand immediately reached for it, and I could feel a bright smile curling up to form two uneven dimples. My hand went over the ridges, reading the colorful description and imagining a multitude of youthful adventures in the galaxy far, far away.

I was so entranced that it took me some time to realize that I was an outsider there. A quick look to my left revealed a weird gaze from a girl about my age, perhaps a little younger. In her hand she clasped a magenta Barbie dollhouse, and as our eyes met I witnessed her confusion. Feeling uncomfortable, I broke off the eye contact,. To my right, a boy of about 12 was focusing on me; he narrowed his eyes as though trying to solve an enigma . I left the blaster and found my father a couple of aisles ahead. I tugged at my father's shirt, asking if he could do a favor for me. When he asked what it was, I walked to the exit of the aisle, and asked if he could grab the blaster for me.

After all, this was the boys' section, and I was out of my place.

What affected me most about this experience was not the event itself — it was the reason for why I felt the way that I had. After all, what matters in a simple toy section? The answer? Everything. And no, this isn't being dramatic.

I had the pleasure of speaking with Sara Mauskopf, a computer scientist and CEO of the startup Winnie. Winnie is a mobile and browser app that can connect parents to fun activities and offer handy tips and tricks, while notifying you of family-friendly entertainment wherever you are. It's exciting, much needed tech in this age where apps are slowly encompassing our lives. Entering the Massachusetts Institute of Technology as a math major, Mauskopf transferred into computer science after taking a course on a whim. Absolutely fascinated by it, she delved deeper and today is shaping modern parenting through Winnie.

Being a female executive in Silicon Valley is often isolating considering the lack of representation at the top of the ladder. That's why Winnie is committed to hiring and employing female engineers — to increase diversity. And when creating such a family-centric product, it's no wonder that Winnie is making strides day in and day out.

One of the key issues we dove into was exactly why more girls weren't choosing STEM as a major or career. Mauskopf stressed her parents' constant support of her studying mathematics or tech-related fields. This wasn't much of a surprise — there's only an infinitesimally small number of parents in the United States who would actively discourage their daughters from studying computer science. But it turns out that that wasn't the problem. What struck me, in fact, was when she explained the more subtle ways she experienced discrimination.

For example, Mauskopf recalled that when she was choosing a college to attend, an older man and friend of the family who had graduated from MIT spent a long time trying to dissuade her from applying to MIT. He told her that MIT would be a lot of work and harder than anything she had ever done. In hindsight, it's fortunate she did attend, as it "wasn't actually as hard as he made it out to be". What's interesting about his statement is you could feel unsure about 'what was behind it'. For instance, one might ask, how would you absolutely know that the statement was biased? Or stereotypical? You could just be hearing what you want to hear. So how do you know, for certain? Well, it's easy. Just ask yourself, what are the chances it would be said to a male of the same age? If you can't easily imagine it being said to a male counterpart, it's probably biased.

Girls and boys at young ages are routinely exposed to gender norms and biases. It's everywhere, all around us, and in every facet of our lives. It's what shapes our society and us as individuals. And the earliest inclination of this can be seen in children's toy sections.

The toy section is the first realm a child is allowed to control their choices and where their choices can start influencing them in return. This is the culmination of early childhood and an introduction to a limited degree of freedom. Therefore, it's fascinating to see how a particular selection affects their thoughts and opinions. In my personal experience, it's always been a bit confusing. I'd be drawn to the toys in the boys' section, embarrassed, for no reason other than I wasn't seemingly fitting in with the rest of the crowd. As more and more manufacturers are slowly eradicating these gender-defined products, more progress is attained. However, Mauskopf reiterated one of her personal encounters with this sort of her bias. Her daughter is only a toddler, but someone recommended a book about a female engineer called Eva the Engineer. However, the book starts out by saying that Eva is bad at math and science.

If you take a look at, say, a Lego section and browse the products, you will see a vast array of occupations and careers being featured. From engineers, to the police force, firefighters, chefs, and others, Lego certainly seems to sell a diverse set of products. But the next time you happen to visit a store, try actively counting the number of females featured in the toy sets. And then, the number of females of color. Not that many in comparison, right? This lack of representation is evident, apparent, and unfortunate if you make a conscious effort to recognize it. But the fact is, most people don't end up noticing it, and instead regard it as the norm in their subconscious.

When toys are one of the first encounters our children have to our culture, it's regrettable that we are already placing them in boxes: Boxes labeled 'girls' and 'boys', with a set of prerequisites and expectations stamped on the outside of each one.

Many of the boys' boxes display a limitless array of possibilities. Browsing the aisles, you can see anything and everything from dinosaur hunter to special agent. The words pressed into the wood are words like 'adventurous', 'daring', and 'brave'.

Outside the girls' boxes we view something different, but it seems ordinary to us. Inside, you can see everything from Barbie dolls, to baby toys, to princess dresses and tiaras. The words pressed into this particular piece of wood are 'pretty', 'beautiful', 'graceful', and 'poised'.

Alone, these ideas seem harmless. But when you combine this with the impressionable minds of young kids, we begin to see that concepts such as these shape them forever. Despite being a strong feminist, I still believe, somewhere inside me, that boys are natural leaders and girls are followers, as the media I have consumed has designated this as normal.

Mauskopf thinks there are a multitude of ways that society discourages girls from entering STEM pursuits and activities. In order to prevent this thinking from reaching her daughter, she "started having to modify some of [her] daughter's books and [ultimately changed] the main characters from male to female so she could see that girls can do things besides be princesses. People will buy [her] daughter princess books...and tell her how pretty she is and so she's getting inundated by the wrong messages." And it's exactly right — we're sending the wrong messages!

Children, male or female, should be praised on ideals such as hard work, determination, and perseverance. They should be encouraged to follow their own aspirations, chase the stars, and pine after their wildest dreams, regardless of their gender. But when we're unconsciously telling girls that the majority of their worth is based on their appearance, we're not cultivating the right kind of inspiration and values. And that's unfortunate, because we're telling little girls that their tiaras and dresses mean more to us than the wealth of their creativity and imagination. This is the crux of our generation's problem: we mean well, but we need to take a step back, analyze the situation, and act accordingly. Sometimes, the things we consider normal need to be reevaluated. Mauskopf's own experiences echo the roots of the gender gap in STEM by actively pointing out what society expects from all of our children.

When young, girls don't look too much into gender stereotypes. The result of this is evident, as many express genuine interest in STEM subjects and hobbies. As I did, many receive or buy science-related games, kits, or items of the like. They participate in classroom discussions, have confidence in their answers, debate with their peers, and have an unsatiated curiosity. Many see themselves on an equal playing field — as they should — and don't doubt themselves because of their gender.

However, as these girls grow older, they start becoming more aware of the world around them. Realizing the expectations of poise and grace society has placed on them, they begin to feel self-conscious of their decisions. Many start to doubt their own places in STEM, observing a lack of female peers around them. As they enter the teenage years, the wanting to 'fit in' and be part of a greater whole captures their desires. This is further amplified by the internal conflicts of set standards and individualistic expression.

This process happens to boys as well, but in a different way. As they mature and grasp the world around them, assumptions of each gender start to be made. Delving into the belief that boys are suited for STEM subjects, many adopt the 'bro culture'.

The 'bro culture' is a phenomenon experienced in the workplace and everyday life where a group of males are seen as 'bros' and part of a special group. Female peers are seen as not being in the 'in', and are treated like outsiders — with the only reason being their gender. These ideas are only further shaped by the use of slang such as 'brogrammer', where the mindset of a college fraternity is implemented in a workplace or similar organization. Masculinity is seen as the ideal, and femininity as weakness. And although many males do not associate with these types of environment, even those at the top are not always immune from 'the mindset'.

Susan Fowler, an ex-Uber employee, would attest to that. Uber is a transportation company headquartered in San Francisco, servicing over 570 cities worldwide. It currently commands the ride-sharing market, where anyone with a phone can be driven anywhere. It's the taxicab of the future, and something both urban dwellers and suburban residents alike frequently benefit from. With revenue upwards of $6.5 billion, it seems that its convenience and ease of use make it a winning combination. There's just one problem — its culture, and specifically bro culture, is one of the worst in Silicon Valley.

Since Uber's release, there have been numerous reports of sexual assault and similar incidences in Uber's cars. In fact, it became seen as unsafe for females to travel alone using the app. But the actions of a few don't represent the intents of all, and I had never thought the company itself to be sexist or discriminating, as these were the actions of their drivers and not necessarily the organization itself. But that changed when I learned of Susan Fowler.

Susan Fowler worked at Uber starting November of 2015. Eager to begin her new job as an engineer, she beamed with energy and brilliance. Uber, at the time, was seen as a fresh and new alternative to traditional taxis, and was steadily increasing its profits and potential. But as Fowler became more and more acquainted with the workplace, she started observing incidents that shouldn't have been left unnoticed. Her new manager starting texting her inappropriate and lewd messages, and as any decent employee would do, she shared them with the human resources (HR) department. Susan wrote in her personal website on February 19th, 2017, that "[she] was told by both HR and upper management that even though this was clearly sexual harassment and he was propositioning [her], it was this man's first offense...and they wouldn't feel comfortable punishing him for what was probably just an innocent mistake on his part."

Despite working her hardest and turning in great work, Fowler also received less than stellar performance reviews from her superiors. When asked about this difference in opinion, she received the unconvincing response that "performance problems aren't always something that has to do with work, but sometimes can be about things...[about] your personal life."

Later, after interacting with a few women engineers at the company, it became apparent that instances such as these were far from unusual. Uber had noticeably turned a blind eye toward this behavior, and professionalism was put in the back seat. She found that it was far from her manager's first offense, and his sexism was rooted in Uber's culture — its bro culture. According to Fowler, when she joined the company in November, they were composed of over 25% women. But when she left in January, that number had dropped to 6%. In Fowler's division (Site Reliability Engineering) alone, at the time of her departure, only 3% of workers were female. But when she asked one of Uber's directors at an event about the substantial gender gap in the company, he simply replied that women needed to be better engineers. An HR representative had disclosed to her that "sometimes certain people of certain genders and ethnic backgrounds were better suited for some jobs than others, so [she] shouldn't be surprised by the gender ratios in engineering." Basically, hidden behind elaborate phrasing, the director was promoting unsubstantiated, sexist, and racist beliefs to support his concept of the ideal, and specifically male, engineer.

These events show that we still have a long way to go when we see companies worth billions still using the same old-fashioned thinking that was disputed years ago. When tech-aspiring girls enter their teen years, and they witness this rampant bro culture within their schools, they slowly start to turn away from the sciences. They fear being the odd one out, and face a fork in the road: either accept the status quo and a lack of peers, or pursue another field where gender ratios are more equal. And unfortunately, many girls avoid engineering and computer science majors in favor of other disciplines.

In 2014, Google released a comprehensive study titled *Women Who Choose Computer Science: What Really Matters.* The report sought to understand why so few women choose STEM majors and to reveal any other root causes for the lack of diversity within tech companies. Amongst the overall criteria, the paper found that there are four key factors influencing whether a girl chooses a computer science major or not: social encouragement, self-perception, academic exposure, and career perception. Social encouragement relates to the support a girl is given via her family or culture. Self-perception relates to her own aptitudes and skill sets that can be used in a career setting. Academic exposure concerns the availability of previous computer science coursework, and career perception is influenced by a girl's view of tech careers and paths. But perhaps the most telling part of the report was the statistics — the cold, hard numbers.

Even though we believe we're progressing as a society when it comes to gender gaps, certain fields lag behind. The Google report found that the number of girls earning degrees in STEM, overall, has increased, but in computer science, it's declining. Google found that "female participation in computer science, specifically, has declined to 18% from a 37% peak in the mid-1980s." And that's concerning when we take into account the sheer number of engineers that are needed today. There isn't enough supply for the demand, and we'll eventually see the consequences of that. But for now, there is an alarming lack of diversity at nearly every tech company in the world — and Google is more than aware of this.

Diversity is great and everything, but so what? What's the point? What's to gain? The answer is everything. We limit our technological advances when we don't actively promote diversity. This issue is two-pronged — it's correlated with statistics and with our own biases. The statistics tell us that less and less girls are entering engineering and computer science, and our biases tell us that's to be expected. But there are certain harms when it comes to preserving the gender gap, and it goes beyond simple ethics.

Let's say you're boarded on a plane. You're sitting in business class, with some sparkling water in your hand, enjoying the view. You happen to be a doctor, and a heart surgeon at that. A vacation in Hawaii lies ahead of you, and you can't wait to take a break from the stresses of your local hospital. But suddenly, the plane starts gaining turbulence, and the overhead announcements tell you to strap in. The yellow oxygen masks come flying down, and the people around you seem frantic. At first, it seems routine and under control, but you begin to realize the plane is going to crash — and it's heading for an unknown island. The plane violently hits the ground, and the only survivors remaining are the passengers. You all agree on something as soon as you assemble — you need to begin a new process of life in order to sustain yourselves before you are rescued. And that might take a long time, as the island is undiscovered. But then you all also come to another revelation: you're all heart surgeons! Now, this is great for patching up and treating some of your fellow doctors, but then, you're forced to create a temporary legal system. It would've been handy to have a lawyer on board. After that, you need to work on growing plants and fruits to eat, and learning what is poisonous and what is not. It might've been helpful to have a farmer or botanist on the plane. And then, finally, you realize you need to start reaching out to the outside world to signal where you are. But you need extensive knowledge of radio signals and sound waves — an engineer would have been very useful had they been with you.

What's important about this analogy is that it illustrates how different people have different skills to offer. Even if we're all taught the same curriculum, every person comes from a unique background and thinks a different way. If all the surgeons had to come up with a temporary system to sustain themselves, they would be great at creating triages and developing natural medical processes. But they wouldn't have as innovative ideas about legal practices, plant cultivation, and signal triangulation that people of other professions would have. And that's exactly why we need diversity: diversity allows us to pool together every unique thing we have to offer, and when we cooperate effectively so much more is accomplished.

But to first understand how to close the gender gap, we need to know where its support is coming from, and where these ideas are originating. There are three main sources: society, individuals, and the bro culture.

Society influences many of our views and beliefs. Where you are raised, brought up, and taught often shapes you as a person. But it's also in the media that we consume on a daily basis. Julia T. Wood of the University of North Carolina at Chapel Hill is a professor researching gender bias in the media.

Wood, in *Gendered Media: The Influence of Media on Views of Gender*, writes that the disproportionate lack of women in film and TV imply men as the societal norm. She argues that females, statistically, are not represented enough in a way that their achievements are valued over their physical attributes. Similarly, Wood persuades that:

> Prime-time television favorably portrays pretty, nurturing, other-focused women, such as Claire Huxtable on *The Cosby Show*, whose career as an attorney never entered storylines as much as her engagement in family matters. In the biographies written for each of the characters when the show was in development, all male characters were defined in terms of their career goals, beliefs, and activities. Hope's biography consisted of one line: "Hope is married to Michael." (Wood 33)

Wood also explains that within the media, there is a correlation between women and dependence, and between men and independence. Women are perceived as unable to care for themselves without a man to help them, whereas men are seen as free-spirited and more than able to take on a challenge. Traditional roles such as caretaking for women and breadwinning for men are also depicted frequently.

Films and television can directly affect our views, whether changing them dramatically or introducing subtle thoughts. But it's the suggestive, recurring patterns that leave an imprint in our minds most of all. After years and years of consuming media, it becomes evident that our biases are shaped and reshaped over and over again. The ideas that entertainment feeds us are part of why we continue to use gender norms and roles — we're used to it, and it feels normal. It seems normal to have stay-at-home moms and male mechanics, but the moment you switch them, it feels a little off. Not necessarily wrong, but off. Like that's not the way it's 'supposed' to be.

Nearly every conscious animal or being on this planet has their own way of communicating. Language is the way we exchange crucial information, learn from each other, and advance our society. When human beings initiated verbal communication around 100,000 years ago, it was one of the most important developments in our evolution. Some of the most popular languages spoken around the globe are the Romance languages. Originating from 'vulgar Latin' or 'common Latin', the Romance languages are used widely across the world. Spanish, Portuguese, Italian, French, and Romanian are the most common, boasting a total of nearly 825,000,000 speakers globally. These languages all have some sort of gender-variant, meaning that they do not contain the word 'the' as English does. Instead, they use either masculine or feminine articles to convey the word. In Spanish, the most spoken Romance language, the singular feminine article is 'la', and the singular masculine is 'el'. This article precedes a noun, and the noun is often referred to either feminine or masculine. However, many of these nouns were often conceived hundreds and hundreds of years ago, where gender bias was commonplace and generally not discouraged. As a result, these nouns are often stereotypically masculine or feminine. '(El) país' is the Spanish word for country, while the word for flower is '(la) flor'. The standard word for genius is '(el) genio', and 'la ropa' is the phrase for clothing. Generally, if you have a group of people in Spanish (or another similar language) who are all female, the group is referred to as feminine, and vice-versa for a group of all males. However, if there is even one male in a group, and the rest are female, the group is referred to as masculine. Even if there are a thousand women, and only one man, the group is still referred to as masculine! The fact that there are many, many more females in a group does not change the rule — the male holds precedence overall. FluentU, a popular online educational service, provides free language resources and help. In one of their articles regarding the grammar of groups, they state that "the masculine gender has more power than the female gender when it comes to making the rules. Although the words have the same value, the male acts as the default leader."

Within this excerpt, the vast majority of people wouldn't notice the layers upon layers of preconceived notion and bias. When a group of languages that are spoken by nearly a billion people around the world are described to assign more 'power' to the masculine gender, or that "the male acts as the default leader", that is how you know there's truly a problem. Spanish is an incredibly beautiful language, but it's doubtful that it's derived from zero biases. However, this has less to do with the actual Romance languages and more to do with the ideas behind them. What's so powerful about language is that it's the absolute best drifter into our subconscious. The way we think, within our own minds, is directly controlled by language. But when our own vernacular promotes biases such as these, it's no wonder that it's ingrained within us. We can't help it — it's literally how we think!

But, as much as our society and language shape us, we equally play a role in defining ourselves, and it's evident in our everyday lives. Let's say you are the head of a laboratory in the city of San Francisco. You have to hire a mathematician to oversee a certain division of the organization. You have to pick between two people for a job that requires extensive mathematical knowledge and application of said knowledge. The top two options are sitting before you, and the only major difference between them is that one is a man and the other is a woman. Now, if I asked you who you'd pick, you'd probably say you couldn't decide. Most people wouldn't believe that they would hire the man, solely on the basis of gender.

But researchers Corinne A. Moss-Racusin, John F. Dovidio, Victoria L. Brescoll, Mark J. Graham, and Jo Handelsman of Yale University released a study in 2012 titled

Science Faculty's Subtle Gender Biases Favor Male Students, and startling results were found. They reached out to the faculty of top research universities, and asked them to rate applications for a laboratory position. Using a double-blind model, 127 people were asked to give their opinion on each candidate. However, the name for each side was randomized — one was male, and the other was female. This was the only difference between the two candidates. Everything in the application was kept exactly the same. When the results came back in, one thing was evident: gender plays a massive role in the perception of your abilities. The team noted that:

> [Faculty] participants rated the male applicant as significantly more competent and hireable than the (identical) female applicant. These participants also selected a higher starting salary and offered more career mentoring to the male applicant. The gender of the faculty participants did not affect responses, such that female and male faculty were equally likely to exhibit bias against the female student…. These results suggest that interventions addressing faculty gender bias might advance the goal of increasing the participation of women in science. (Brescoll, Davidio, Graham, Handelsman, Moss-Racusin)

It's important to understand that these applications were completely identical — there was absolutely no difference at all besides the name on the front of the page. This type of bias isn't solely groupthink — it's ingrained in most of us. It's this ever-permeating individual bias that's feeding into the groupthink, and allowing the groupthink to feed back to it. It's a positive feedback loop, of sorts.

What's even more interesting is the examination of faux progress. Malcolm Gladwell is a Canadian journalist, writer, and speaker. You might know him for his popular titles *Blink* and *The Tipping Point*. Gladwell's popular podcast, "Revisionist History", reinterprets events of history that might have been overlooked — i.e., whose significance have never been thoroughly understood. In his first episode, "The Vanishing Lady", Gladwell speaks of Julia Gillard, Australia's first female prime minister. Sounds progressive, right? We're always used to seeing the advancement of women in power as a good thing — which it is. But then, Gladwell goes on to talk about the concept of moral licensing.

Moral licensing is defined as doing something good in order to improve your perception of yourself but then giving yourself 'license' to do something immoral, as you've already 'proven' you are moral. For example, when Gillard was first elected, it seemed that females had finally permeated the upper branches within the Australian government. Sexism is gone, they said! Misogyny is now nonexistent!

The truth, however, is all her election did was give license to many who had voted for her to pursue sexist views.

As they had already voted for her and 'proved' their progressiveness, they now had the right to spew misogynistic statements and keep to their traditionalist views. Gladwell speaks of a similar study done with the election of U.S. President Barack Obama in 2008. It was found that many of those who had voted for him, claiming their 'progressiveness', held controversial racial beliefs. Because they had voted for a black president, it seemed okay to hold racist views.

The same applies here — Gillard was now the victim of rampant sexism and discrimination, despite governing from the highest chair of the land. In 2012, Gillard gave a passionate address within the Australian Parliament speaking out against this behavior, and focusing on the sexist comments made by her campaign opposition, Tony Abbott. Gillard's speech echoed throughout the world, with prominent women such as Hillary Clinton applauding her message. And yet, Abbott still won the election.

But what's the significance of moral licensing? It's often what's advancing the gender gap. For instance, if we encourage more women to join in tech professions, but then don't create inclusive environments, we're utilizing moral licensing. If we decide to hire a female for a STEM position as she is thoroughly qualified, but then behave inappropriately around her, that's moral licensing. If we support a female executive at our company because she can lead us down the right path, but then crack misogynistic jokes with the 'bros', that's moral licensing.

The group is made up of individuals, but we, as unique people, influence the culture of the group. If we're not making a conscious effort to correct our biases, then we're no closer to changing the damaging 'bro' culture that's rooted in tech.

Think back to *Jimmy Neutron* and the subtle biases that are apparent throughout the show. Has there been a Jessica Neutron? Or a variety of TV shows with incredibly strong female leads, whose scientific knowledge is showcased front and center — and not their love interests? CBS's *The Big Bang Theory* is a slightly more popular example of how the bro culture, as Professor Julia T. Wood implied, permeates our media and beliefs.

In *The Big Bang Theory*, physicists Leonard Hofstadter and Sheldon Cooper live together in an apartment in Pasadena, California. Working at Caltech, they're Mensa-certified geniuses, with plenty of scientific know-how up their sleeves. Their intelligence is contrasted by their weak social skills and lack of common sense. Joined with aerospace engineer Howard Wolowitz and astrophysicist Raj Koothrappali, the four men personify geeky, social awkwardness. But not all of the show's characters are male. For example, the waitress Penny is a series regular — but she doesn't have the sheer academic knowledge her cohorts have. Leslie Winkle is an astrophysicist whose abilities are shadowed by her description as "former girlfriend of Howard and Leonard". Neuroscientist Amy Farrah Fowler's role in the show is centered around dating Sheldon, as she joins the group only after they meet. Bernadette Rostenkowski's place in the show is concisely described as Howard's girlfriend and later wife. Emily Sweeney is a talented dermatologist and all, but that's not stressed — her relationship with Raj is, though.

What these descriptions tell us is that although many of these women are just as academically gifted as their male peers, their intelligence isn't showcased often. Their defining traits aren't that they're astrophysicists or neuroscientists or dermatologists. It's that they happen to be dating one of the guys — one of the 'bros'. No recurring, STEM-oriented females on the show haven't dated one of the guys — but the same can't be said vice-versa. *The Big Bang Theory* is a show that's so culturally relevant, but one that keeps feeding us this culture, in and out of tech — this environment where the men are in the 'in', and the females, albeit academic peers, are not.

Very few television programs, whether for kids or adults, feature women with sharp intellect. Although you might find some here and there, rarely will they be a featured character. This tendency is especially common in Hollywood, where hit movies such as *Terminator* and *Die Hard* champion hypermasculinity and aggression. Only in 2017 are we starting to have more strong female characters, but there's still the catch-22 of moral licensing — one might ask, if we introduce more female characters in our films, is it okay to lessen attention on the lack of representation? Or must we continue to fight for further equality? I say the latter should be our standard; moral licensing shouldn't be the norm, but the rare exception.

When we're showcasing limited diversity in the media, whether it be in movie or TV, we're telling our children that this is normal, and it's okay. This impacts both boys and girls, and only augments the 'macho' culture, cultivating it from childhood. When a belief is formed in early years, it becomes even harder to eradicate it. Similarly, in 2014, nearly 82 years after its creation, Lego released a set of figures depicting females in STEM activities and pursuits. Before this, there wasn't a single Lego toy, out of hundreds and hundreds, with this kind of message.

Looked at singly, these are all relatively small problems, but such things are never discrete events. They work together to form one narrative, a narrative that doesn't only affect tech but the world itself. Wherever you find yourself in the world, whether it be STEM, politics, or the liberal arts, this narrative will always play, because it speaks within each and every one of us.

But you and I, with help, can fix that.

This bias has continued for long enough, and it's time for a solution. And the new generation of girls are it. We're strong, we're smart, and we've grown up in the information age.

We're thoroughly acquainted with consumer tech — we were the first ones explaining Snapchat, posting on Instagram, and making YouTube a commercial hit. It's time to now be the driving force behind the products we consume, and shape the next generation's aspirations and goals. Let's be the ones creating the next Snapchat, developing the next Instagram, and meeting with venture capitalists for the future YouTube. With the array of possibilities ahead of us, let us take a chance by diving in together — fighting the gender gap, one girl at a time.

We can start by acknowledging the issues surrounding us and coming together to offer solutions. The most important step in fixing a problem is to realize there is one in the first place — let's educate ourselves, and that alone will be a tremendous step. So read all you can, and research what you've missed, because knowledge is power.

If you're like me, and enjoy the sciences, don't let the culture or lack of peers turn you away. We're the modern equivalent of 'patient zero', all trying to close the gap. We'll be one of the only ones for a little while. But, that'll soon change, because we'll set a precedent that others will follow. It will take time, but it will happen.

You can start in the smallest ways. For example, participate more in your science and math classes at school; take a computer science course if you have one. Ask questions and understand the answers. Read about STEM articles you find interesting, and maybe pick up a coding book. Try to build small websites for fun using basic HTML and CSS (programming languages which nearly every website has). If you disagree with a peer in school on an answer (male or female), stand up for what you believe. It's okay to be wrong — it's miles better than being afraid of failure.

You can also pursue STEM on a larger scale. Try to start with solving a problem. Are there no computer science or engineering classes at your school? Petition for them! Start clubs, school organizations, and bring like-minded girls around you the same opportunities. Maybe aim to educate others on the benefits of picking up tech skills.

If you're interested in gaining funding or publicity, check out organizations such as the National Center for Women and Information Technology. NCWIT awards a select number of high school girls the Aspirations in Computing award for dedication to tech pursuits. It's also a great way to seek out mentorship from a woman currently working in a science-related field.

If you'd like to learn more about women in the computer science space right now, visit the Grace Hopper Conference hosted by the Anita Borg Institute. It's hosted annually for three days and is home to some of the brightest minds in tech right now. Keynote speakers are often prominent names in the field, and the positive environment at the convention reverberates through all. Although attending is a bit expensive, they do offer scholarships and ways to reduce the cost overall. If you're passionate about computer science and the future, it's an amazing way to get acquainted with the people who are advancing it.

It's a fantastic time to be in technology.

New fields like artificial intelligence and machine learning are advancing every day, and companies like SpaceX are pushing the limits of software in space. Old technology is quickly being superseded, and new discoveries are constantly being found. STEM is the way our world is going to advance — it's almost a sure bet. But in order to create that world, that world of progress and innovation, we need diversity, and we need you and me. Girls like you and me are going to bring another perspective, vision, and path.

So let's get to work!

OVERCOMING OBSTACLES

It's clear that there's an epidemic playing out in front of us. And it's also clear that something needs to be done about it. But perhaps this is the decade where our generation finally turns the tables and not only breaks the barriers, but the wall as well. It begins with us, and firstly, with the perceptions of ourselves.

After years and years of conditioning and societal bias, it's clear that gender-biased views affect both men and women, and specifically how they influence opinions of themselves and each other. While it's true that many girls are confident in their abilities, it has been found time and again that self-assurance plummets during the teenage years. It could be attributed to changing mental states, but also to a sudden awareness of cultural norms and beliefs. And it's phenomena such as the bro culture in tech that only reinforce traditional and misogynistic views, driving away the bulk of female talent in the STEM field. This is directly causing a lack of diversity in the tech workplace, *leading to an innovation deficit*. We need tech feminism, and we need it now.

But, girls, we're keeping ourselves away from tech too — it's not just the pervasiveness of the 'brogrammer' culture. In fact, we might have the largest part in it. And if we want equality, and we want diversity for all, we're going to have to overcome some obstacles, beginning with our own selves.

The bro culture, in schools, clubs, workplaces, and executive boards is alive and well. But let's get one thing straight — that doesn't mean it's accurate in its thinking, especially when we're talking statistical data. This is especially important, because we need to believe and internalize that it's invalid if we're going to overcome any obstacles. Professors Janet Hyde, Sara M. Lindberg, and Amy B. Ellis of the University of Wisconsin at Madison, and Marcia C. Linn of the University of California at Berkeley have come to the same conclusions. In the study, *Gender Similarities Characterize Math Performance*, published in 2008, the researchers found that STEM performance in schools is nearly equal when girls and boys start on equal playing grounds. The scientists' study originally set out to validate or discredit previously held beliefs that females are weaker at STEM subjects — one that both teachers and parents may hold. When so much of the justification behind 'men being better engineers' is based on academic prowess, it's important that we check our facts. And the facts tell us otherwise — in math, a core subject in STEM, scores are nearly equal. Equal! Not only does this debunk any sort of sexist rationale, it also delivers hope to any girl with a belief that her gender is a weakness. Acknowledging the discrepancies in general thinking and scientific results, the researchers noted that although "stereotypes that girls and women lack mathematical ability persist and are widely held by parents and teachers...for grades 2 to 11, the general population no longer shows a gender difference in math skills." With math being a core component of STEM, this revelation is game-changing. When so much of our general thinking is based on outdated knowledge, it's a breath of fresh air to finally see the truth come out.

Even though this is great news, it's important to note that it's also been this way for a while. Nothing has changed in terms of our capabilities. But when it comes to the brogrammer culture, the truth doesn't matter — it's the belief. And when the facts do not hold to a particular way of thinking, 'they should be taken with a grain of salt'. This belief is what's dangerous, as it's present everywhere and in many facets of our own lives, and doesn't require any justifications. There's no rationale needed to be sexist — it's a free country, and you can think whatever you'd like to. Such a belief is what convinces people to adopt certain biases and discriminatory thoughts. The belief is what allows a vast array of people to rationalize the gender gap as beneficial for society. So when Lian Bian and Andrei Cimpian of the University of Illinois at Urbana-Champaign and Sarah-Jane Leslie of Princeton University's Department of Psychology conducted a study to research gender biases concerning academics, it was no surprise what they found.

The youth are the future, and the principles of the future can be found in our youth. Aiming to study how and when gender stereotypes affect children, the researchers collected data from a total of 240 kids. It's no secret that from an early age we absorb certain pieces of information about the other gender. We start forming our own opinions and beliefs, and they gradually mature as we grow older and understand more things. We may end up passing some of these beliefs to our own children, causing a generational hand-me-down of potentially outdated and discriminatory information. But what the scientists wanted to figure out was when exactly did these biases started to manifest — did it start at birth, or the beginning of consciousness? Did it start when they began speaking? Did it start when they entered school, and if so, what grade and age? It'd have to start somewhere. Specifically targeting the gender gap in STEM, they wished to know when children (both male and female) started associating brilliance, a trait that corresponds to success, with males.

They selected 96 children of ages five, six, and seven to participate in the study. To begin the experiments, they read a story to the kids. Lin Bian, one of the researchers, told the groups of a fictional person she works with. She went into this person in great detail, but stressed the fact that "this person figures out how to do things quickly and comes up with answers much faster and better than anyone else. This person is really, really smart." Bian reiterated once more their massive intellect, careful to not reveal any other details of her co-worker. Focusing again and again on the sheer brilliance of this person, the kids listened diligently, thoughts ticking away in their receptive minds.

After story time, the children were shown four different pictures of adults. Two of the adults were women, and the other two were male. The kids were asked to point out which person they thought was the person in the story that they had just heard, and given as much time as they wanted. The majority of five year olds, male or female, were very likely to pick a person of their own gender. For instance, many of the girls picked the women, and vice-versa for the boys. The team derived that at this age, societal norms and biases haven't quite formed yet, at least in most children. The girls still associated brilliance, academic potential, and leadership as a gender-neutral or female trait. Their response was personally aligned with themselves, and their projections were positive for the most part.

That changed very quickly when the six and seven year olds were tested. As Jess Hennessey, a writer covering the experiment, wrote:

6- and 7-year-old girls were much less likely than 6- and 7-year-old boys to associate brilliance with their own gender. This suggests that changes about children's ideas of intelligence occur rapidly, and that gender disparities in beliefs about intelligence are evident by age 6.

In the space of only one year, many of these girls had quickly reverted their opinions of self-confidence and assurance, yet the boys experienced no such withdrawal. The team also conducted a separate study composed of nearly 150 adults, with similar results. What these conclusions tell us is that it only takes a simple belief, and a wildly inaccurate one at that, to shift the mentalities of our youth. When a way of thinking has been formed at merely age six, it's almost impossible to fully eradicate. At that point, it's a part of you, and you'll never truly erase it — which is why the adults displayed very similar biases. Thoughts developed during early childhood not only endured till adulthood but had taken an increasingly resilient hold in the intervening years..

When it comes to the gender gap in tech, it's important to note that much of the struggle isn't direct conflict because the discrimination that's causing it is very subtle. And although much of this bias is spread by 'brogrammers' and people of the like, it's us, the girls, who are allowing it to spread by believing it. It'll be difficult, but if we begin to rid ourselves of biases and start gaining self-confidence in STEM areas, we've already solved half the problem. And there's evidence out there that not only supplements this belief, but encourages it as well.

In 2017, Google, the most innovative tech company in Silicon Valley, was hit with a scandal of incredible magnitude. An engineer of theirs, fairly new to the company, had released an internal manifesto that many believed to be anti-diversity and anti-inclusionary. The manifesto was ridden with 'facts' claiming that women are "neurotic", and because of "biological differences", men are superior engineers and scientists to women. There were two things about it that made it extremely dangerous:

- It had an air of faux reasonableness – he seemed as if he was telling the truth in a calm and composed fashion
- It further advanced the misogyny in the brogrammer culture

Recently, I included in my personal project "A Girl in Tech" (www.natasharavinand.com) an entry on this issue. The following is an excerpt of this particular entry:

For those who aren't aware, the tech world has recently been shaken to its core. Since its inception, there's always been a rather large gender gap in the STEM workforce – in fact, only 29% of all STEM workers are women. Within that 29%, there are hardly any racial minorities represented (African-American, Hispanic, Native American, etc). As a result, the community has been under extreme pressure (for good reason) to encourage more women, and women of color, into tech jobs. This is especially crucial, considering the pay gap between technical careers and non-technical jobs. More diversity equals more perspectives, which in turn result in more innovation.

Google Inc. has been actively searching for ways to encourage more women to matriculate into computer science degrees. In fact, they've written up numerous reports, conducted several studies, and set up a multitude of programs to motivate young girls to pursue science. They've found that the hostile and misogynistic nature of tech's bro-culture is a prime factor in keeping women out of STEM.

Despite being one of the most progressive organizations on Earth, Google is still plagued by those perpetuating myths disguised as fact; bias disguised as pseudoscience.

James Damore is one such person.

A former Google engineer, Damore has written a full, 10-page "manifesto" on Google's misguided views concerning the gender gap. Women, according to him, are just 'better' at some things, like being "agreeable", and men are just 'better' at complicated, systemic programming.

So, on behalf of all the teen girls and women whose dreams are continually repressed, undervalued, and underestimated due to our gender — here's what I have to say to you, Mr. Damore:

I wish you realized that your words relate to many hateful, misguided people in this country. That many men do, in fact, agree with what you say. But despite working in the most progressive company in the world, I wish you realized the complete rubbish you have used to make your 'points'. I wish you realized how much work you've just undone in Silicon Valley, because you've shifted the silent bias of many to explicit discrimination, and you've made misogyny okay. I wish you realized that your actions have not only brought to light your underlying sexism, but also your implicit bias you described yourself in your 'manifesto'.

And you may be wondering, what could a 16-year-old girl possibly know about this? And you'd be right — to an extent. I'm not nearly as old, 'wise', or infamous as you. But I do know one thing that you don't – in fact, me and the other 29% of your peers.

I know what it feels like to be underestimated. I know what it feels like to be ignored. I know what it feels like to be valued less. I know what it feels like to always try to prove yourself. I know what it feels like to not be in the 'in', or the bro-culture you and your friends are unwittingly feeding into.

As a person of color, the system is already against me. Being female makes that even harder. And now, if I want to go into technology, it feels like I'm bringing a knife to a gunfight — I can't possibly come out of this unscathed. And that's a feeling you'll never know, because you can't possibly understand. You couldn't possibly understand.

You say that "the distribution of preferences and abilities of men and women differ in part due to biological causes" and you claim that "these differences may explain why we don't see equal representation of women in tech and leadership".

But what if I told you that it's not that black and white? That not everything can be solved by you, being one person? That maybe, you're part of the problem, and not even close to the solution?

What if I told you of the millions of high-school girls each year who make up but a small fraction of their computer science or engineering classes? Or the hundreds who are harassed on StackOverflow by your like-minded 'bros'? Or the thousands of your peers who routinely have to prove themselves, holding themselves to a higher standard, because people like you automatically assume less of them?

What if I told you of Emily, whose real name I won't reveal? What if I told you that Emily had an immense passion for robotics, and participated in every competition she could find? What if I told you that Emily was an incredible student, continually excelling at math and science? What if I told you that she had an intellectual gift, whose mind was made for systemic thinking.

What if I told you that Emily was continually degraded by her male peers? That when they looked at her, they saw nothing but a pretty little thing, incapable of anything except for objectifying? That when they looked at her code, and it turned out to be better than theirs, they'd steal it and pretend that they wrote it all along? What if I told you they'd "mansplain" even the simplest things to her, and would cast her away from the group? What if I told you that Emily decided against entering STEM due to her gender, and that the tech world has lost an unimaginable gift?

What would you say?

Well, as you did in your 'manifesto', you'd claim that you aren't talking about specific cases, but women on average. You'd call Emily spineless, saying all she had to do was 'deal with it'. And you'd bring in your army of facts, raging toward the reader, all of them trying to pick and point and persuade you.

You've tried to protect the validity of your views by claiming "on average" this or "on average" that. After all, when someone points out a counterexample, you could just default to saying that you're talking about the bigger picture. But Mr.

Damore, you aren't looking at the bigger picture. You're utilizing blatant stereotypes you've adopted over the course of your life to support your sentiments. Nothing you have said is considered absolute fact, and that may be an important disclaimer to add. But it's too late now.

You claim to have a solution to all this. And hundreds have read through it. You've gotten what you want: a platform to spread your bottled-up, repressed views. But guess what? You're missing the point.

When you claim that "biological differences" are what make men better than women at some things, you're using zero credible science. Even if I picked out, printed, and delivered the plethora of studies and research done that discredits your view, put a bow on it, and placed it on your doorstep, you probably wouldn't get the point. Your supporters wouldn't get the point.

The archaic, obsolete nature of your argument makes it astonishing that you are (or were, I should say) an actual Google engineer. You're using completely debunked pseudoscience to support your incredibly misguided claims.

If only you knew of the obstacles women face every day. If only you knew that the entire system, in every facet of our lives, is against us. If only you knew of the lack of genuine representation we see in tech, the media, and the government, as well as the discrimination and objectifications we put up with on a day-to-day basis. If only you knew that maybe the complexities of the whole world aren't black and white, and that they're much more than what meets your eye.

The minute you condense 50% of the population into a singular stereotype, with no knowledge of the hardship they face each and every day, you are directly feeding into the culture that Silicon Valley is itching to distance itself from — the more you feed into the sexist, misogynistic views you're (indirectly, or not) championing.

And you know what's the most disturbing thing, Mr. Damore? You don't even know that you're being explicitly, wholly, and absolutely sexist. You just see this as the simple truth, and you wonder why everyone else can't see how right you are. When you're together with a few of your 'bros', and all complain together, it seems that the whole world is against you.

But maybe, just maybe, if you looked closer at the lives of your peers, you might see how much harder the journey to the top has been for them, compared to you. You might check your privilege. And instead of spreading your sexist beliefs, you'd cooperate with your female peers to find a real solution.

And maybe, just maybe, I'm a prime symbol for the "Ideological Echo Chamber" that you speak so critically of. But you know what? I'm okay with that.

Because I know, in a hundred years, history will not look fondly upon your convictions.

I include this excerpt to show how the most ambiguous and dangerous displays of sexism are the ones that exude faux reasonableness. But keep in mind — anyone who claims that women, due to "biological differences", are inferior to men, isn't backed up by science. They are cherry picking facts to supplement their own arguments, and are not looking at the general scientific consensus.

On the contrary, Daniel Voyer and Susan D. Voyer of the University of New Brunswick's Psychology department published their study, *Gender Differences in Scholastic Achievement: A Meta-Analysis*, in 2014, detailing how gender affects school performance. In previously released studies, the Voyers acknowledged there had been correlations between gender and subject proficiency — in short, it had been found that males are stronger in mathematics and females in reading comprehension. These results have permeated general opinion and are now regarded as fact.

Drawing data from nearly 500 samples, the duo set out to analyze school marks and grades, relating them to gender and investigating the connections between the two. This way, the results they compiled would be even more accurate than any individual study done. The schools chosen were elementary, middle, and high schools, as well as undergraduate and graduate programs, comprising countries all around the globe. Regions such as North America, Scandinavia, and Africa were represented to ensure proper diversity.

What the Voyers eventually found was surprising indeed and quite contrary to individual studies of the past. When looking at overall academic performance, females generally had better marks across the board, and when looking at subject-by-subject examples, there was still a female advantage. The Voyers emphasized that:

[Their analysis] revealed a consistent female advantage in school marks for all course content areas. In contrast, meta-analyses of performance on standardized tests have reported gender differences in favor of males in mathematics...and science achievement...whereas they have shown a female advantage in reading comprehension ....This contrast in findings makes it clear that the generalized nature of the female advantage in school marks contradicts the popular stereotypes that females excel in language whereas males excel in math and science. (Voyer)

The data, presented in a lengthy and detailed meta-analysis, described all the findings, detail by detail. The overall conclusion was that there was, no doubt, a female advantage when it came to grades and marks in school. These "gender differences favored females in all fields of study", regardless of whether the course was STEM-based or humanities influenced.

It's obvious that intelligence isn't entirely based on grades themselves — they're but a letter or number grade signifying the success of your completion of the course. Many factors go into a person's overall mark: their attendance, participation, performance in examinations and knowledge of the material. What grades can tell us, however, are which students are most effectively analyzing what the course asks of them and succeeding in that particular realm. From hundreds of samples, the Voyers were able to discern a larger female success rate, signifying that the generalized belief of gender strengths is incorrect. There isn't some overarching power working to make sure that males are good at STEM and girls are good at humanities, and there isn't any disproportionate evidence claiming this as well. The truth is we're all basically equal, and some people don't necessarily like that. But do and think as you may — it's the truth, supported and verified.

So now that we know, for certain, that we're capable of taking this on, let's look for some inspiration. And what better inspiration than figures of the past?

There are quite a few household names who've hailed from the technology community — many Americans are aware of Mark Zuckerberg, Bill Gates, and Steve Jobs, because they've all contributed in some way to their lives. Perhaps, when they wake, they refresh Facebook on their iPhone, search for updates, and later head to their Microsoft computer to check emails. These men are all incredible technological pioneers, but who was the first? Who can be considered the very first computer programmer? The answer? Ada Lovelace.

Ada Lovelace was born Augusta Ada King-Noel, Countess of Lovelace, on December 10, 1815. An English mathematician, she was fascinated with numbers and their purposes. But she was interested in more than that. She wanted to create something bigger than herself, something that would amaze and further society.

Her father, Lord George Gordon Byron, had married her mother Anne Isabella Milbanke, and was promised a child: namely, a "glorious boy". However, on the 10th of December, he found he had been bitterly wrong. His wife had given birth to a daughter, and the Lord was displeased, to say the least. Additionally, Ada was the only legitimate child of Lord Byron, which meant he had no direct heir. Given that England has traditionally been a patriarchal society, this is understandable but unsettling. Soon after Ada's birth, Lord Byron departed England, eventually perishing in the Greek War of Independence some time later. All the while, Ada's mother tenderly supported Ada's growing interest in logic and mathematics. Ada was a revolutionary in the making, with numbers and logic being her sword.

In her teenage years, her mathematical skills would rise exponentially, and her talents did not go unnoticed. She soon made acquaintance with Charles Babbage, a famed English mathematician interested in Ada's advanced abilities. Today, he's considered the father of computers, and for good reason. In the early 1800s, he was working on his Analytical Engine — a mechanical, general-purpose computing instrument, which he deemed was fit only for number crunching and calculating. Ada, however, was skeptical. She felt that computers could do much more than simply compute values, and decided to do something about it. In a lengthy collection of notes she held concerning the Engine, Lovelace wrote the world's first algorithm. Essentially, she coded the first computer program! Her program calculated the Bernoulli numbers: rational numbers created from an exponential generating function. But the revolutionary part of this was computers could now be programmed to carry out a specific task, and then programmed to execute another one. They didn't have to be built for specifically one purpose. This is the core of all programming: to solve a problem, and then another one after that. It's never just one!

If we look to modern times, her vision has now come true. Computers are rarely used for raw calculation. In today's age, we're even looking into the realm of studies like artificial intelligence, where computers can simulate human thoughts and actions. In fact, there are even programs out there today which can take in chapters of a book and write a chapter for you, just following the author's style! Plot and everything!

Today, Lovelace is famous in the world of computing. Her hardship and perseverance through all her obstacles have inspired millions to take up the science of programming. Ada

Lovelace Day is celebrated annually on October 13th. Through thick and thin, Lovelace revolutionized the world. Margaret Hamilton did the same.

Born Margaret Heafield Hamilton on August 17, 1936, Hamilton was always fascinated with numbers. Raised in Indiana, she traveled to the University of Michigan and later attended graduate school to pursue abstract mathematics and philosophy. When she joined MIT in 1960, she was mostly developing software to predict weather patterns. But later she would be asked to join the SAGE Project, a MIT endeavor to aid America in the Cold War.

The '60s were a tumultuous time for the United States and the world in general. With the threat of nuclear weapons, fallout had become a real possibility. Nations everywhere were petrified of the possibility of warfare as it would have been unprecedented in its nature — of a kind g no one had ever seen before. Anything was up for grabs, and 'doomsday' theorists became very popular.

Hamilton and the rest of her team were directed to develop software to defend from Soviet attacks, and to even identify unfriendly aircraft. The code written there had a direct impact on American maneuvers and plans, greatly aiding the war effort. In this show of leadership, the National Aeronautics and Space Administration (NASA) offered Hamilton the job of programming software for the most famous set of missions ever conducted: Apollo.

The Apollo missions were designed to push humanity to its greatest limits. Since time immemorial, we've always dreamt of setting foot on the moon. When we looked to the stars on clear nights, it was always the moon shining bright back at us. So this landmark would be our first major venture into our galaxies. Its goal would be to set humans on the moon in manned mission and advance findings in unmanned operations. In the famous Apollo 11 endeavor, astronauts Neil Armstrong and Buzz Aldrin made "one giant leap for mankind" when they took the first ever steps on the surface of the moon. All of this, however, could never have happened without the software designed by many — and Hamilton in particular.

After Hamilton's part in the SAGE projects culminated, she began working for NASA to program in-flight software for the Apollo missions. Hamilton rose to become the Director of the Software Engineering Division at the MIT Instrumentation Laboratory. She and her team worked tirelessly, day after day, constantly editing and perfecting their code. It's even been seen that Hamilton juggled her roles as a mother and lead scientist — she'd bring her children to the labs and then code while they played. Hamilton truly excelled in her time as a software designer, and the fruits of her labor were sweet: her code is what got us on the Moon in 1969! Without engineers like Hamilton, we may not have landed on the Moon as quickly as we did, and we may not be seeing the same avenues for space exploration that we do now. For example, modern-day companies like SpaceX are setting their sights on the red planet: Mars. Experiments are even underway to explore whether humans could survive on the red planet. But we must remember the people who helped us along the way, and Hamilton in particular.

Back in the 1960's, STEM was very much a 'boys-club', with an astonishing lack of female engineers present (a culture which has improved only slightly today). Hamilton's name had all but disappeared from view, with little to no recognition for the vast amount of code she contributed to our nation and for her part in the success of the space age. . In 2016, however, a long-due recognition materialized when she was awarded the Presidential Medal of Freedom, signifying to all that in this era, women *can* be anything and *can* be recognized accordingly for their achievements. However, the movement for equality within tech wasn't yet fully realized. That came later — with Anita Borg.

If you're well-established in the computer science community, you know exactly who Anita Borg is. Born in Chicago on January 17th, 1949, Borg had always had a passion for mathematics. Interestingly, she was not always set on pursuing programming; she picked it up at a later job. Eventually earning a Ph.D in computer science from New York University, she worked numerous programming projects, eventually landing a position at Xerox. Her greater passion, however, didn't lie necessarily in coding. Rather, it was in diversity and in the movement to correct the gender gap in tech.

Borg was a fervent supporter of equal representation in STEM, and an avid feminist. Remarking once that "women will change the corporation more than we expect", she pined for a world where women were paid and regarded the same as men. And instead of sitting on the sidelines waiting for progress, she rose up and created change.

In 1987, Borg attended a convention on computing principles named the Symposium on Operating Systems Principles. One of the most well-regarded assemblies in computer science, she was eager to meet like-minded people who shared her passion for computing. However, she was shocked by the amount of women there — or lack thereof. Nearly everyone was male!

At the Symposium, however, Borg was able to meet the very few other female attendees, who were as shocked as she was at their low numbers. The lack of diversity was apparent, but no one seemed to be as concerned about it as they were. Even at the Symposium, a prestigious gathering, there was a fervent bro-culture. To combat this, together they created Systers, a mailing list specifically optimized for technical women. Articles on the list mainly related to the topic of women in tech, but the group didn't just create a mailing list. They also were activists, campaigning for Mattel to change the microchip on one of their female dolls. The doll was selling on the open market, and many girls had already heard the phrase "math class is hard" from it. Considering the myriad of evidence explaining why this is damaging, Systers truly did make a difference — Mattel pulled the microchip in '92.

Perhaps Borg's most influential achievement was what came in 1994. Borg and a colleague decided to create the Grace Hopper Celebration of Women in Computing. An annual conference that would exclusively cater to females in tech, the event was named for none other than the pioneering computer scientist herself.

The convention today boasts an attendance of thousands, with tickets selling out within minutes online. It features talks from famed keynote speakers, technical and career sessions, as well as live presentations and demos dedicated to computing and STEM. There are ten specialized tracks: academic, technical, student, steering committee, Birds of a Feather sessions, technical theme, career, conference theme, industry, and the invited technical speakers' track.

In 1997, Borg created the Institute for Women in Technology. The overall goal of the organization was to increase the number of females in computing and the amount of technology produced by them. Borg's vision for the future was that the field of programming be 50% men and 50% women by 2020. Even though this may not be reached in the near future, Borg would be hopeful in knowing that there are girls like you and me still here, eager to make it come true! And today, there's now a new generation of role models, and a new generation of women in tech.

As we keep advancing further and further as a society, even with our flaws, we still manage to make some progress. There are women out there right now, in the field, truly making a difference. One person can't solve a problem as generational as this; it'll take a community. So in order for us to break that wall, let's look at some women today who are crashing down its brick and cement.

Marissa Mayer, former Yahoo! CEO and President, climbed to the top of the tech ladder piece by piece. Born on May 30th, 1972, Mayer grew up in suburban Wisconsin. After harboring an avid interest in the human mind and collective thought, she enrolled in Stanford University, initially taking pre-med classes but switching to symbolic systems. Later, she would pursue a Masters in computer science, and specialize in the field of artificial intelligence.

Artificial intelligence, for those who are unfamiliar, is a realm of technology dedicated to imitating the human mind. You might think of Hal from *2001: A Space Odyssey*, or even Johnny Five from *Short Circuit*, but believe me, its applications go far beyond simple movie magic. For example, artificial intelligence is often used in customizing a device's news feeds or advertisements; a program can pick up on your searches, your likes, and your dislikes, and use that information to suggest more relevant items to you. In addition to this, artificial intelligence is also prevalent in robotics, with more and more companies investing in projects that intersect the disciplines. The United States Defense Advanced Research Projects Agency (DARPA) has recently created its very own humanoid robot, named Atlas. Atlas is bipedal, and primarily used in search-and-rescue operations. It's AI allows it to carry out these tasks efficiently and completely, with no loss of human life. Artificial intelligence is also directly impacting our domestic economy, as more and more occupations are being motorized to expedite the process of manufacturing.

So one could say, back in the 1990s, that Mayer got a head start. After graduation, she had a plethora of opportunities sitting in front of her. She chose to join Google, and was employee #20 — their first female engineer! She assisted with the launch of Google AdWords, a system that aids advertisers in client demographics, while helping the design of the iconic Google search page. Mayer directly oversaw numerous Google products, including Gmail, Google Maps, and Google Images, to name a few. After teaching multiple classes at her alma mater, Mayer was awarded the honorable Forsythe Award from Stanford University. And in 2012, she was appointed President and CEO of Yahoo!, a noted media corporation. Sheryl Sandberg, similarly, has also climbed her way to the top of the tech field.

Odds are, if you've ever been on the internet, you've heard of Facebook. And if you've heard of Facebook, you've also heard of its founder, Mark Zuckerberg. Even though Facebook was created by one person, it was grown by a team of people, working with a vision in their mind and a cause that enveloped them all: to connect human beings on a singular, all-encompassing platform. And on that team was Sheryl Sandberg.

The current COO of Facebook, Sandberg is one of the most influential tech executives of our time. After graduating from Harvard Business School, she worked for Larry Summers, the United States Secretary of the Treasury under the Clinton administration. Once Republicans took over the White House in 2001, Sandberg ventured to Silicon Valley, the nation's tech capital. After working for Google for a couple years, she met Zuckerberg at a party, who hired her later for the role of Chief Operating Officer. Today, Facebook is worth upwards of $400 billion, complete with 1.86 billion active users. That's nearly a third of the total global population! It's by far the world's largest social network, boasting a user base practically unrivaled. Its success has made it one of the top companies in the world, and it's often considered one of the tech trifecta: Apple, Google, and Facebook.

During her tenure at the company, Sandberg has made strides in pushing for equality in the workplace. In 2014, Sandberg backed the Ban Bossy campaign along with Jennifer Garner and Beyoncé. The movement intended to ban the word 'bossy' from the workplace — a term that's often used to demean women in executive and leadership roles. In addition to this, she's also written the acclaimed *Lean In: Women, Work, and the Will to Lead,* and subsequently created an organization of the same name. *Lean In* explores women in management roles, the struggles that inevitably come with it, and ways to advance equality in the workplace. Sandberg believes passionately in the impact childhood experiences can have on adult biases. In *Lean In,* she explained that "from a very early age, boys are encouraged to take charge and offer their opinions" and that:

> Teachers interact more with boys, call on them more frequently, and ask them more questions. Boys are also more likely to call out answers, and when they do, teachers usually listen to them. [However] when girls call out, teachers often scold them for breaking the rules and remind them to raise their hands if they want to speak." (Sandberg 26)

She's also delved deeper into how this affects later life, offering explanations for why women tend to hold so few managerial positions. She explains that:

> [Taking] risks, choosing growth, challenging ourselves, and asking for promotions...are all important elements of managing a career. One of my favorite quotes comes from author Alice Walker, who observed, 'The most common

way people give up their power is by thinking they don't have any.' (Sandberg 80)

In addition to her activism, Sandberg has been featured prominently in the media, and is repeatedly ranked as one of the most powerful women in business.

Sandberg is a fantastic example of someone who is advancing women in STEM without actually being a STEM-focused person. Her background is in business, yet she's one of the most influential figures in the tech field. All in all, it goes to show how there are many different avenues computer science can take you — from business, to politics, and even social media.

Mogul is an award-winning platform where millions of women around the globe can share information, knowledge, and advice, all through one cohesive social experience. Community users post on various hubs ranging from politics, to cooking, to pop culture, to technology and coding. Located in 196 countries, membership ranges from Pakistan, to Malaysia, to the United States, and even the Middle East. But Mogul is more than a place for discussion; they're also partnered with the United Nations, and other international organizations, where they help provide 62 million girls free access to education. They have created a curriculum used by 18 million women around the globe, with courses based in tech, entrepreneurship, and emotional intelligence. And to top it off, they've created an expansive network where enterprising saleswomen can market their products to a variety of interested clientele. But it makes you wonder – just how did this organization come about?

I recently had the pleasure of chatting with Tiffany Pham, the founder and CEO of Mogul, as well David Pham, CPO/CTO, about the roots of the company. Mogul was founded a couple years ago when Tiffany was placed on Forbes' 30 Under 30 Media list. Throughout her life, Pham had been incredibly involved in entertainment and information access. At CBS, she worked with one of the Presidents of the organization in managing a variety of different properties at the network. In addition, she was working with the vice mayor of Beijing in order to unite both the U.S. and China in terms of the cultural gap in entertainment. Moreover, Pham had co-produced *Girlfriend*, a film that starred a man with down syndrome; it debuted at the Toronto Film Festival in 2010.

But once she was placed on Forbes' list, Pham received a flood of emails and messages from women around the world. "I would read every single letter and write back, but I wondered: what if we had a platform where millions of women could share insight and knowledge with one another?" she inquired. And from there, she set out to create her own dream: a place where women could learn, share, and grow with other women. But it was not easy. Developing a site like Mogul would require advanced coding skills, something that Pham was not particularly familiar with. "But I asked, maybe I could teach myself how to code Ruby on Rails and help these women with their lives." And after some time, Pham said, she had built the first version of Mogul. Within its first week, Mogul had launched to over a million users.

David Pham, her brother, agreed that it was a genuine success. And he's firmly rooted within Mogul's cause. "We want to give women every bit of support in order to become better every day", he said. "To help them achieve the things they want in any shape or form." And Mogul's been doing that incredibly; women from South Asian countries like Pakistan have written to them, claiming that in their land, a woman's life is centered around marriage: but on Mogul, she sees that she is so much more than that.

He also shared how we might not always recognize gender inequality. "From the very beginning," he outlined, "there's a lot of societal influences that shape both men and women. I'd like to think about it as a domino effect: imagine you have a single domino, and from that single domino, you have these two dominoes. And depending on which domino it hits, the impact is huge."

Likewise, Ms. Pham agreed that gender equality is of utmost significance. "It's important to enable women to speak up and have the courage to share their ideas and insight", she articulated. And the platform has been critically important in bridging societal divides and barriers to create a better world.

"Mogul has inspired women across different cultures, letting women unite across certain themes", Pham said. "For example, a young woman in London started writing pieces on the platform about body positivity, regularly. Her pieces inspired a user in America to write about body positivity, and she herself had inspired girls in China to realize body positivity is important. Moreover, they wanted to bring that empowered theme to China."

Mogul has been a revolutionary platform for women, and it still continues to do so. The company is already branching out into several more divisions, which include the acclaimed Mogul at Work, Mogul Learning, Mogul Redefined, and Mogul Studios. Each works to better women's lives across the globe, and each is increasing its influence day-by-day.

The creation of Mogul shows us three things:

1. Women with a cause can create, develop, and fight for their dreams.
2. Cultural and societal divides can be remediated with tech.
3. With cooperation, teamwork, and understanding, it is possible to tackle the challenges each gender faces. Moreover, it is possible to overcome them.

If there's anyone who has overcome failure to go on and achieve incredible successes, it's Reshma Saujani. She once ran for political office; namely, as a representative to Congress. Campaigning in the great state of New York, she spent over a million dollars, and ended up receiving less than 7,000 votes. She was beaten in a sheer landslide, and failure seemed to be the only option. After all, she'd lost, and she'd lost dramatically. Once a rising political star, they claimed. But it seemed that she was now yesterday's news.

Not quite so.

An Indian-American, Saujani was born in Illinois, and attended the University of Illinois at Urbana-Champaign to study Political Science and Speech Communication. She would later attend Harvard and Yale Law School to earn a Masters in Public Policy and Juris Doctor (J.D.), respectively. Saujani would work in corporate law before running for office, and even worked pro-bono in some cases. But as she delved deeper into her professional pursuits, she started to realize one common thread: the lack of women.

Nearly every professional field has a disproportionate amount of men at the top of the ladder, and we've explored why this is. Saujani believes this is a sort of epidemic, and traces it back to its source: young girls. She has mentioned time and time again of a 'bravery deficit', a term she coined herself. A bravery deficit, according to her, is apparent amongst our young girls. In essence, we're sacrificing our girls' potential by teaching them to be flawless, while inhibiting their aptitude in taking risks and trying new things. Her insight has been incredibly valuable to the tech community, with insightful observations and noted credibility. She's previously claimed that this deficit starts at childhood, and that:

> Most girls are taught to avoid failure and risk. To smile pretty, play it safe, get all A's. Boys, on the other hand, are taught to play rough, swing high, crawl to the top of the monkey bars and then jump off head first. By the time they're adults and whether they're negotiating a raise or even asking someone out on a date, men are habituated to take risk after risk. They're rewarded for it. It's often said in Silicon Valley that no one even takes you seriously unless you've had two failed startups. In other words, we're raising our girls to be perfect and we're raising our boys to be brave. (Saujani within her acclaimed TEDTalk "Teach Girls Bravery, Not Perfection")

And as a society, it's exactly true. We encourage our boys to play it rough, to stir up the pot, to ruffle some feathers. To reach for the stars, and pine after success. With girls, it's a constant struggle to stay perfect, stay poised, and stay graceful. To keep that dress pretty and perfect, and offer a smile when appropriate.

Saujani has previously spoken of a typical story that occurs routinely in clubs across the country. A class will be given a coding assignment, and one girl will come up to the

Facilitator asking for help — apparently, they're not able to complete it. The Facilitator comes over to the computer and sees a blank screen. It seems that the girl has just sat, doing nothing, without even trying the problem first. You might be quick to pass judgment. But if one pressed 'undo' a couple times, you would see that the girl almost had fully functional code: it just wasn't perfect. And as Saujani describes, it was perfection or bust.

It's events like these which truly bring to light how serious this epidemic is. Alone, they might seem harmless, but they're not separate issues. They're all connected in this interlocking web of conditioning and crippling perfection. Overall, we're lacking in the courage to overcome those obstacles in the way of our success: the same obstacles created by the sexist biases of our society. Now, not everyone in our communities is sexist. We've come an incredibly long way from the 1950's mindset. Discriminatory views are slowly starting to wither away. Just not fast enough. So, we need to catalyze that process.

Saujani took it upon herself to do just that. After her defeat in the New York congressional race, it seemed like there was no other chapter to turn to. But instead of ignoring this reality she had been observing for some time, she decided to do something about it. It was time, she realized, to repair our bravery deficit, and replace it with a bravery surplus.

In 2012, she started the national nonprofit Girls Who Code. Now, if you're a girl who's interested in computer science, you've probably heard of Girls Who Code. It's essentially an educational organization dedicated to closing the gender gap by empowering young girls to learn coding. Girls Who Code boasts a membership of over 40,000 girls, with 10,000 clubs in communities across America. In the club setting, there's normally a Facilitator who oversees the growth and development of the girls' coding skills. Using fun, easy-to-learn activities, the girls slowly but surely learn important programming concepts in a safe environment. Much of the time the participants have no coding experience and study the material alongside their friends in schools, churches, libraries, etc.

What's important about the Girls Who Code experience is that it takes one very important thing out of the picture: fear of condescension and inadequacy. Often, as I've experienced, there's a significant bro culture in schools. It's not, by any measure, just limited to the workplace. Many girls around the country routinely undergo some sort of devaluing conversation with their male peers, who want to be the top dog when it comes to math or science. It can happen subtly, as it normally does (phrases such as "you didn't know that?", "that's not right — let me show you how to properly do it", or "where did you even learn to code?") or more indelicate. And when many females, at the middle school or high school level, first experience this, it often takes coding out of the picture for them. It's the systemic bias of it all that turns them away, and not necessarily the individual comments.

But Saujani really has struck the gold with Girls Who Code. With 'sisterhood' and bonding activities, the girls learn to trust one another and learn more about each other. One of the principal ideas of the organization is that it's not acceptable to demean someone for a lack of knowledge, or to show off for the purpose of making others feel inadequate. This removes the fear of being ridiculed, and allows complete beginners to join a club and feel comfortable. There are zero prerequisites, other than a hardworking attitude and an eagerness to learn. Girls who may have not initially picked up programming now have an opportunity to do so. And most importantly, it's fun, so more join!

As the clubs progress, they're allowed to pick their own projects to build. The girls venture into more advanced programming concepts, and some have even gone on to build functioning apps and websites. According to the organization itself, upwards of 60% of its students are seriously considering a computer science major/minor in the future.

But Saujani definitely has obstacles ahead of her. The Advanced Placement (AP) Computer Science test is often the first encounter many high school students have with computing in their own classes. But according to UC Davis, not one girl took the Advanced Placement (AP) Computer Science test in

Wyoming, Mississippi, or Montana in 2014. And that may seem debilitating to Saujani's goal: 1,000,000 women in the field by 2020. Hispanics did not participate in 8 states, and African-Americans did not take the test in 11 states. But, as is the case with many causes, Girls Who Code still needs more time to make an overwhelming impact. And when it arrives, it is sure to shake the status quo.

When the vast majority of consumer products are being bought by women, it's imperative that we start building them! Women, overall, use social media 500% more than men, so we need to be creating the next Instagram, Facebook, or Snapchat. Products for men and women, made by men *and* women. It's basic feminism, equality, and common sense. We can do it. We've overcome harder things before.

But first, we have to undo this concept of crippling perfection. We're conditioning our girls to be flawless, faultless, and ultimately insecure. We're not teaching them that it's okay to fail sometimes, and that it's okay to not always be right. We're not teaching them that the only thing that isn't okay is a fear of trying new things — a fear of risk and their own free thought. That's the kind of encouragement we should be promoting: a mindset to reach for the stars, to break down any walls between you and your dreams. To have a goal and set your sights on it, any distractions blurred, given no attention. To be treated with the same respect and regard as your peers.

Women will have an undeniable influence on future innovation. We have slightly different skill sets and talents, and when men and *women* work together, great things happen. It's a matter of cooperation and collaboration, making for a more productive and advanced society.

It can even be broken down into a very simple equation: gender diversity = an abundance of perspectives = more innovation = a better future.

Diversity really is key here, because it's what the tech community desperately needs at this particular moment. We're at a critical point in time — we're building the most cutting-edge tech we've ever seen. It seems as though *Back to the Future* has come alive; we're working on humanoid robots, setting up Mars colonies, and creating the most realistic artificial intelligence ever known to humankind. It's truly an exciting time to be alive, and it's even more exciting to be making our dreams come alive. But the tech we make right now is going to determine the kind of future we have, and we need an all-inclusive one. It's imperative that when we're creating products that affect all humans, most humans are represented in the creation of said products.

Let's say you traveled 500 years into the future, where our civilization has experienced an exponential increase in technological aptitude. We're now able to create faux bodysuits, and with the click of a button, transcend our own forms. We can now take the identity of another, and this allows us to escape our old lives and live longer. Your curiosity piqued, you decide to try it for yourself. You pick a brand new suit, get situated in the machine, and let the science do its work. Something about particle physics, they said. All you're thinking about is how incredible this is.

After your transition, you decide to take a stroll in the park. Well, it's not really much of a park anymore. They've upheaved nearly all the trees for residential buildings, and everything gleams a metallic shade. You breathe in the cold air, and continue on your merry way. But as you walk farther and farther, you start feeling different. It's not a good kind of feeling either; in fact, you feel like you're going to collapse any moment.

And it turns out that you did. Next thing you know, you wake in a hospital bedroom with a doctor standing beside you. He has his surgical robot next to him, implanted with the newest biotech AI that is offered. He tells you that you've had a rare complication, and nearly every one of your body systems is malfunctioning. However, he says, there's no need to fear. I have an amazing team of oncologists, and we're ready to help you. Just oncologists, you ask? He affirms. But, you inquire, if it's all my body systems, should we also be getting a cardiologist in here? A neurologist? A gastroenterologist? Wouldn't they all add valuable input? No, no, he says. I can assure you, he adds, that we'll be enough. You nod, and while quavering, fall back into the chair.

Now, that's a bit of an unrealistic example, but the point is there. When collaborating to find a solution to a problem, it's vital to draw from many perspectives. Consistently following the same train of thought might solve the first issue, but when confronted with a different one, it will be inadequate.

The same thinking can be afforded to gender diversity. Being born a boy or girl significantly impacts the rest of your life. From biological differences, to particular interests, to how people might treat you, it indirectly affects everything. As a result, males and females may hold very different perspectives on the world, but when they come together they can form the complete picture. It's like building a puzzle; if you only have half the puzzle, you may be able to make out the image, but you won't be able to solve the problem properly.

It's really this array of perspectives that makes diversity so important. Gender diversity is critical, but so is racial diversity. Life experiences, overall, of an African-American woman probably differ from those of an Asian man, and the views of a Hispanic man might be different to those of a white woman. Race nor gender defines you, but it does affect some of your own thoughts and beliefs.

When you have this expansion in diversity, you lead to innovation. As more and more people from different walks of life collaborate to create something, it's likely that it'll be very different than if one specific people developed it. This cooperation is what encourages healthy competition and compromise, with all sides representing their consumer base. So, I think I speak for many when I say that closing the STEM gender gap is beneficial to all. It's beneficial for our domestic and global markets today, our students of tomorrow, and our little girls of the future. And once we light the match, we ignite the whole cause. We just need that initial spark.

We cannot afford to turn away any more female talent. At a time when progress is crucial, we must have our best thinkers and engineers on our team. What we create today defines tomorrow, so let's make sure we're starting on the right foot.

There are already moral implications rooted within the brogrammer culture, but, as seen, there are economic and development ramifications as well. We need to make sure we're on the right side of history here, and although that may seem dramatic, it's true. Tech has been what advances our society: nearly every milestone of humankind can be related to a technological invention at that period of time.

Diversity simply adds dimension to an idea or a thought. People have uniquely different minds, think dissimilar thoughts, and critically reason in their own ways. *Through the Labyrinth: The Truth About How Women Become Leaders* by Alice H. Eagly, a Professor at Northwestern University, and Linda L. Carli, an associate professor of Wellesley College, offers another perspective on the matter. Politics, for an absurdly long time, has been a male-dominated realm, due to age old gender norms.

Men, and white men specifically, disproportionately comprise the majority of elected seatings. In 2017, Congress is supposed to have reached its most diverse year. And that's true — but the catch is, women only make up 19% of the House of Representatives and only 21% of Senate positions. At this time, we have never had a female president, in our 250+ year history.

Carli and Eagly studied the effects of a more women-led political sphere. Particularly, the results of an alternate kind of leadership. Did gender, altogether, really make a difference in legal proceedings? Was there no major variation between a male-dominated office and a female-inclusive one? Their results were spectacular and very telling.

There happened to be a noticeable disparity in the way men and women govern, mainly due to the attitude assumed. Men tended to want to lead the discussion, and direct the issue wherever they chose. Generally, it was a less egalitarian atmosphere, where people generally saw a strict hierarchy of political influence. However, when the pair examined the governing style of the women, it was wholly different. Women were much more likely to open the floor up to debate, and more inclined to adopt a less rigid approach. In their book, they detail the more distinct differences they observed, including that:

> [In general] women adopt a somewhat more democratic or participative style than men. Similar findings emerged

in a study of committee chairs in state legislatures. The female chairs, more than their male counterparts, acted as facilitators rather than traditional 'take charge', directive leaders. (Carli & Eagly 126)

Women often tended to look to their peers for guidance, leading to a more collaborative atmosphere. This collaboration is what can best foster the optimal political atmosphere. Often, you might be aware of politics as convoluted, in disarray, with disagreements and stalemate occurring far more often than progress. Effective communication can easily change that, and it's something we desperately need in an era where partisanship delays growth. The researchers continue, providing noted perspectives from those within the chambers themselves. For example, Carli and Eagly note that one might:

[Consider] a colleague's description of Christine Quinn, Speaker of the New York City Council: 'She has injected more democracy...into the Council. Every single council member has a say in the budget. Every single council member has the ability to fight for their constituents.' (Carli & Eagly 126)

Politics is the principal way we govern our lands, our proceedings, and our society. It's essential that our representatives are doing their part in creating a better world for all. This isn't just about the United States — this applies worldwide. If we're not adopting more compassionate and collaborative ways to lead our Earth, we're failing in our own responsibilities. And when we don't promote diversity in politics, and when we consider it to be an 'old boys' club', that's when we run into some problems. Because at that point, we aren't looking to the wellbeing of our future; we're looking toward traditionalist biases and limits. This is the moral implication: we need partnership between peoples, and we need strong communication. When gender diversity can provide us that, the onus is on us to adopt it. That's why it should be every political figure's role to promote an equal 50% of women in elected positions; not just because it's right, not just because it's healthy, but because it is needed. It's absolutely needed if we want to promote a more progressive future for our children, and for our little girls aspiring to be President. We need change.

And the way you can start making change is to challenge the status quo. Challenge what sexist biases say of you, and challenge it with a passion. Don't view discriminatory and demeaning statements as a reason to not pursue your dreams; use them as the incentive. Turn every wrong into a right, and inspire your peers. Never fire back — the long battle is often tedious, but the most effective. STEM can take you everywhere from programming, to aerospace, to writing, to business, and even to politics. Whatever path you choose is up to you — and you only.

And the earlier you start, the better. If you have an avid passion for STEM, that's great! Just an inkling? That's great too! Delve deeper into it, and see if you like what you see. There's a good chance that you just might. It may seem that you can't make much of a difference on your own. But Rome wasn't built in a day, and true progress is never achieved overnight.

If you enjoy STEM activities, then the most important thing you can do is to not fall off the bandwagon, so to speak. It's very common for girls to be as interested in STEM as boys at an early age, but once the teen years arrive, that disappears quickly. Instead, acknowledge the gender gap and the brogrammer culture, and hold your own. The best way you can do this is the simplest: don't give in! Stay in tech, and stay in STEM — arguably, if more and more girls did that, we'd be approaching 50% equality in no time. If your friends enjoy STEM as well, learn with them! Make it fun. Learning should never be boring, or just memorization. Build cool projects, and create new things. Try to solve a problem in your daily life, perhaps, by engineering a simple device. It's great, educational fun, and is an absolutely crucial step to take.

There is no reason to be intimidated by your male peers. There may be times when you feel inadequate or inexperienced next to them, especially if the bro culture is present. There may even be demeaning phrases or 'humblebrags' being thrown around. And some may, as they say, just be in good fun. But what's important to note is that you're just as capable as they are, and science itself proves that. There's no apparent difference between males and females in terms of STEM aptitude — it just isn't there. Don't let the systemic bias get to you; I know, easier said than done. But this is the challenge of a generation, and we'll eventually overcome these obstacles.

It is also imperative that you pursue what you choose to do. Let's say you are fascinated by robots — go and build robots! If there's an excess of boys in your school's robotics club (as there was in mine) still try to work within that environment. If you want to learn more on the side, try getting together with your friends and starting your own organization. It doesn't have to be something elaborate. It could even be Monday evenings building Lego robotics. The important thing is that you're taking steps to increase the number of girls in STEM. Do what you want to do, whenever you want to, even if you're the only female there. Think of it this way — you'll be a pioneer. Ada Lovelace had virtually no peers as dedicated as she was, yet today she's known as the mother of computing. Grace Hopper had just started her studies a decade after women had won the right to vote. At that time, discriminatory and sexist behavior was still looked upon as normal. Yet, despite all the hardship, she still revolutionized the world and became a pioneer of programming. Her and Lovelace's contributions are the reason I am able to convey this message, and the reason you will be able to, too. Be a pioneer, be a thinker, and be unapologetically yourself.

And perhaps, the most crucial thing: never stop learning. Wherever you are, whenever it is, for how many years you live — never stop learning. Knowledge is what makes life so much fuller. It's what offers context, wisdom, and intelligence. Knowledge is the path to freedom, and freedom, ultimately, is the path to fulfillment. It's absolutely vital that you never feel the need to stop reading, tinkering, and absorbing information to progress yourself. Never let anyone take that gift away from you, as it certainly is the most important one.

There's a three-step process that I call the 'Three C's'. The Three C's is supposed to be a comprehensive yet doable plan for communities across the nation. In essence, it's going to help our girls stay in math and science activities, while bringing awareness to the issue itself. The first step to solving a problem is to admit it exists, for if it is never openly addressed it can never be fully solved. That has to be undertaken before any process, with all the truths of the gender gap being brought to light. Although it might seem that technology is a niche sector, this is a conversation that truly belongs in people's homes. The tech created tomorrow needs to be all-inclusive. If we don't start making the change now, we will see the fall-out, the consequences, at some point in the future. We might not see the effects today, or tomorrow, or even the day after that. But the fact is, when it arrives, it'll arrive quick. And suddenly we'll be wondering where we could've stopped it — when we could've promoted the right things and curbed the issue before it took hold.

The first part to the Three C's is Change. Seems simple, right? Not necessarily. The process of changing our mindsets and attitudes on gender norms and biases is not a week-long, month-long, or even year-long process. In fact, it's not even a decade long. It's going to take generations to fully rid ourselves of gender expectations; but the quicker we start, the closer we get to that reality.

We must Change our views on normalized gender roles. The first step is the media. Movies, TV shows, magazines, books, and social commentary — these are all sources of information for us. What we read and hear directly affects what we believe. When we're constantly confronted with gender-specific toys, books, and stereotypical characters in our entertainment, those caricatures start to become real. If we start representing what men and women are truly like — without all the rigid masculinity and expectation of female perfection — then we're showing our children an example of what is the truth. And when this occurs, generation after generation, one by one, we'll see in the near future a radical change in thought. Our kids will learn to view each person they meet as a person — no preset expectations due to their gender. Boys will be able to play with dirt trucks or cooking sets; girls will be able to dress in princess gowns or play with Nerf guns. And most importantly, all of these situations will seem normal. And this normalization is what's truly important, as it eradicates any discriminatory bias by designating everyone as equal beings, with similar interests and pursuits.

We can all play our part. Anytime we see something that has gender-stereotypes, or is gender-defined, we can call it out. We can draw attention to its root cause. We can teach our children and our peers why it's wrong, because many don't realize it in the first place — it's normal, after all. By taking these steps, we're tackling the issue at its heart. The most important thing you can do is to bring awareness, as everything else will follow.

If you see someone making a sexist joke, comment, or remark ("all in good fun", or not) bring light to it. It's uncomfortable, tense, and awkward, especially if it's at a social gathering. But not saying anything simply adds to the culture of how this is acceptable. We've progressed so much as a society; surely sexism can find its way out of our comedy.

If you see organized discrimination happening, in your school or workplace, don't stay quiet about it. One of the characteristics of the bro-culture is it's systemic prevalence. If you see someone, or a group of people, holding someone to a higher standard due to their gender, or commenting inappropriately on their looks, don't be afraid to say something. Often, people will stop and think hard about their actions when an outsider brings attention to them. If you can get a few people to pause, analyze the situation, and change their behavior, you've done good work.

Call for mentorship programs for girls in schools and women in industry. These support centers and aid will make a dent in the miscommunications of the tech sector. Give young girls a sisterhood to learn with, and give working women peers to discuss, connect, and develop with.

Try campaigning to get gender-specific toys and items out of your local department stores or shops. It's routinely the little things that affect us so much. Consciously, we don't realize it, but that's not what matters. Our subconscious is what's absorbing these details, and shaping the way we think while it's at it. If you notice a particular TV show or movie is showcasing insulting and demeaning actions toward females or a race, cease supporting that program by not viewing it. Alternatively, support media that is gender-inclusive (award-winning movies like *Arrival*, *The Hunger Games*, *The Help*, and *Wonder Woman* boast incredibly strong female characters). Lastly, we need to Change the way women are currently shown in the media by increasing our representation. These movies have pioneered incredible literary characters into the mainstream realm, but they're but a small fraction of overall media creation. Instead of portraying stereotypes of women, let's aim for more realistic depictions of ourselves. Let's give society something to show: the true us, imperfect and all, but in a way, as perfect as we possibly could be. And we might just be looking at a Jessica Neutron, coming to screens all over the country.

The next step of the Three C's is to Cooperate. Rarely is progress achieved alone, and, after all, it takes many to accomplish some of great scale. Collaboration is key, especially in tackling an issue that has so many intricacies and so many perspectives. We can start the Cooperation progress small; in communities, towns, and small cities all over the world. Each of us can work with families and schools to open up our girls' exposure to STEM subjects and pursuits. Often, the problem is not necessarily that these girls aren't interested. Rather, it's that they don't even know these options exist! Let's try to open up discussions about the sciences, inspire them, and encourage them to follow their dreams — whether they are in STEM or not. We'll bring attention to the gender gap, one girl at a time, until we have a soaring rate of female engineers dedicated to reaching 50% equality in the tech workplace. This can start by motivating girls to participate in their regional science fairs, or perhaps partake more in STEM discussions in class. We can open up conventions specifically for young girls interested in the sciences, while providing fun activities to do and watch (all science-related, of course!).

We must also make it a conscious point to fund more fledgling, female entrepreneurs. The startup culture is a sort of tech phenomenon — in Silicon Valley, it's as common as finding a Wi-Fi connection. The startup is what allows young, ambitious engineers to innovate, develop, and ultimately sell to make a fortune. Some of the most successful companies to date have been startups: Google, Snapchat, and Facebook, to name a few. Now, they're collectively worth about a trillion dollars. Just for some context, that could pay the salary of 18,000,000 teachers, or run Congress for over 10,000 a year. Because of the potential of a successful startup, it's important to look at how female entrepreneurs are doing in comparison to their male peers, given the bro culture and alpha male mentality present in entrepreneurship. Harvard Business Review recently released an excellent study on how venture capitalists (those who provide seed money for fledgling entrepreneurs) view men and women differently when dealing with funding. This is an incredibly important point: how these people see these women plays directly into the amount of money they receive and the resulting potential for success. If the VC can appreciate your ambition, you might be looking at a lot of cash. This might make or break your chances at becoming the next Instagram. Alternatively, if a VC does not take an interest in you, your shot at fame might just be over. So HBR released a Swedish study of how VCs view the average male and female entrepreneur. Now, it's important to note that these entrepreneurs have very similar qualifications. The result of these studies is not the result of a male entrepreneur being more accomplished than a female one, but simply a gender-bias one.

The males were often described as "young and promising", their short tenure in the industry being viewed as daring and beneficial. The females, however, did not have such an advantage. Their "promise" was instead viewed as "inexperience". A man would be characterized as a "very competent innovator [who] already has money to play with" while a women would be defined by her appearance, with VCs using descriptions of "good-looking, but careless with money". Sometimes the VCs even contradicted their beliefs only because of an entrepreneur's gender. For example, the female entrepreneur could be illustrated as "too cautious and does not dare", designating caution as a negative trait. However, the VCs detail the male entrepreneur as "cautious, sensible, and level-headed". From these conclusions, it's clear that there's a massive double standard occurring in the venture capitalist world. Women are expected to do everything perfectly, but when they're doing everything perfectly, and conforming to this idea of rigid perfection, suddenly they're doing something a bit too perfectly, and now it's a negative action. On the flip side, men are held to a much easier standard, as they don't have anything to prove. The result is an unfair fight, with the challenger never being able to triumph due to a system of injustice.

So in order to counter events like this, we need to start supporting more female entrepreneurs, specifically those in the technological sector. Bustle, a popular media site created for women, has taken incredible steps to combat this sexism. Recently, they partnered with the Flatiron School, a coding boot camp based in New York City, to fund promising women with a cause. Their proposal was deemed the 'Women Take Tech' initiative, with the goal of supplying $100,000 to aspiring female web developers. A few already chosen have outlined their plans for the future. One comes from an entertainment background, and would like to fund her own company to create apps and websites for aspiring performers. Another is a talented musician and teacher who would like to explore the intersections of the two disciplines. She hopes to create free music education with the software she will develop. Programs like these are what encourage more women to pursue technology, and it's worth it. By recognizing a problem and Cooperating with their community to solve it, the Flatiron School and Bustle have truly made their mark on these women's lives.

What Bustle also succeeded in doing was publicizing the issue. By making the article and funding widely available on their website, they were able to bring to light the issue at hand. And that's exactly what we need to do when we Cooperate with each other in our own communities: we need to publicize the issue! In history, there have been a great deal of problems, some serious, and some trivial. But nearly all of them have been solved by drawing attention to the injustice, publicizing it, and making people aware. We're not evil at our core — sometimes, we just don't know what's going on in our world, as we can only see it from our perspective. But if we, collectively, try to educate others on what's going on, we can close the gender gap. And we'll do it much quicker than if we chose not to talk about it.

The final part of the Three C's is to Commemorate. A great deal of causes have had their share of pioneers and role models, and that's exactly what we need to provide to our little girls. We must make Ada Lovelace, Grace Hopper, and Margaret Hamilton the household names they deserve to be. The average adult in America might not have any idea who any of these inspirational women are, and that's part of the problem. We must give our girls a precedent to look up to, because they will not be the first women in STEM nor the last. Inspiration and hope is what ignites the passion of a generation, and simple Commemoration can achieve that.

By celebrating their lives, achievements, and advancements for society, we're revolutionizing the way girls might see their future. We must also acknowledge their struggles in climbing the tech ladder, and the discrimination they faced while venturing upwards. After all, the most inappropriate way of dealing with obstacles of the past is to ignore them. We must make sure our little girls know the hardship they went through, but most importantly, how far they soared once they took success into their own hands.

Closing the gender gap will hardly be an easy solution. It won't take days, weeks, months, or perhaps even years. But progress can never be achieved by the impatient, and despite the difficulties, we must march on. We have the strength, knowledge, and tenacity to do so, and that's what we'll continue doing. It's just a matter of time till we overcome all the obstacles and the wall comes crashing down.

ADDRESSING UNIQUE CHALLENGES

A few years ago, my family and I visited an old Chinese restaurant within an even older area of Los Angeles. We entered the expansive space, complete with bright decor and ornamentation. Bronze statutes filled the room, each one unique, depicting a certain historical or cultural event. Painted above the fray of the top counter was an array of dragons, breathing orange and yellow across the boards. A friendly face soon greeted us, and we were directed to our table, menus placed in front of us and drinks already set. As I looked up, I observed the plethora of little novelties around us, until I saw the massive painting a bit far away. From a distance, I would've picked it to be 50 or 60 feet from us. It detailed a normal day in China, presumably in ancient times, with the paint itself looking aged. Women were pictured picking and separating rice, the men were building some sort of home or hut, and the children ran and played with a small ball. It was a quaint little scene, and a phenomenal piece of decor. After the meal, I walked up to the painting to examine it more carefully. However, it turns out it wasn't a painting, singular. It was a collection of paintings, set up in such a way that from afar, it might seem to be a single entity.

The gender gap is a bit like an illusion. From far away, it seems as if you've got it completely figured out. It seems simple, as if there are only a few properties defining the problem. But few things are ever simple, especially in an issue as complex as this. You could choose to simplify it, as I have tried. However, it is important to note that if we only focus on the big picture, we may be solving the wrong problems by not looking at its intricacies first. Often, people will look at the gender gap and see an entire gender-related issue — which it is. But it's not just that, as it's composed of many demographics and isn't just limited to women as a whole. Asian and white women are joining the STEM workforce at steadier speeds, and in the future we might see the equalization of diversity in the field. But we shouldn't be divulging all our resources on encouraging more Asian and white girls to pursue STEM. We need to be motivating them and providing adequate supplies for their pursuits, but we simply cannot spend the entirety of our efforts on majority women. We need to be focusing them on minority women.

America is the land of immigrants, the sphere of opportunity, and the nation of promise. The premise of our country has been to provide the American Dream: the idea that anyone, no matter your race, gender, or religion, can achieve individual success and personal fulfillment of whatever magnitude. If you take a stroll in Los Angeles, as I have, just by walking a couple miles, you can find yourself in a plethora of Mexican neighborhoods, Koreatown, Chinatown, Thai Town, Little Italy, Ethiopia, and India — just to name a few! In New York City and San Francisco (and nearly every major metropolitan region in the U.S.) there are similar hubs of culture floating around one another. If you happen to immerse yourself in one of these areas, you might seem as if you've traveled to the country itself. Each little 'town' is complete with authentic eateries, clothing shops, and cultural experiences, with its residents fully embracing their own heritage and the haven of the States. It's an awe-inspiring case of generations intertwining by embracing the American Dream, while offering some of their own history and wisdom.

But all too often, we're not seeing the diversity of America within the demographics of tech. 85.3% the STEM workforce is either Asian or white — which is absolutely astounding. These ratios aren't at all proportional when you hear that, according to the U.S. Census Bureau, non-Hispanic whites make up about 61.3% of the U.S. population, and Asians make up just 5.7%. But if the tech field was truly racially balanced, we would see about equal percentages in the workforce as we would see in our country. Now, the reason for this may be the result of cultural pressures and norms, or an abundance of opportunity. The fact however is that only 6.5% of those in the tech sector are Hispanic, and even fewer are women as well. This is apparent despite Hispanics being 17.8% of the population. African-Americans have a similar problem – they're only 6.4% of the STEM workforce, but 13.3% of the overall nation. We're seeing a serious lack of diversity, and the numbers back it up. We can't just be campaigning for gender diversity: we need to start urging more Hispanic and African-American women, specifically, to join the crusade against the gender gap. Without them, we don't truly have the demographics that we need.

In 2016, Jens Manuel Krogstad of Pew Research Center published a few pieces of information central to the growth of Hispanic immigrants in the United States. Pew claims that the total Hispanic population in the States had reached 57,000,000 in 2015 — its peak. And from the years of 2000-2014, Latinos made up 54% of America's overall growth, becoming a quintessential figure in the domestic sphere. Krogstad also noted their quick expansion throughout the nation, writing that Hispanics "drove at least half of overall population growth in 524 counties that had at least 1,000 Latinos in 2014." It's evident, especially in certain areas of the U.S., that Latinos have an extremely strong footing and prevalence. After all, many have migrated here since the dawn of the 1800s, even securing citizenship to this day. But this expansion doesn't translate into universality, especially in highly technical fields where the presence of Hispanic women is virtually nonexistent. There's a lack of role models, visionaries, and technical educators who are committed to fighting this. The unfortunate thing about it all is that if any young Hispanic or African-American girl opens a science textbook and turns to the 'important scientists' section today, it's unlikely she'll find anyone who looks like her among a sea of white men.

A few years ago, the U.S. Department of Education released a publication titled *Hispanics and STEM Education*, intending to report Latino participation in the tech sector. The article covered everything from degrees awarded to Hispanic students, projections of job increases, and a plan to encourage more Latinos into STEM. The Department found that in the 2009-2010 academic year, only 8% of all STEM degrees and certificates were earned by Hispanics. In graduate, doctoral studies, only 3% of STEM degrees conferred were to Hispanics, with results being similar in Masters programs. This all continues as professions such as biomedical engineer project to increase by 62%, with computing jobs close behind. The initiative proposed by the Department of Education was heavily reliant on former President Obama's encouraging actions. The report stated:

> A clear priority for STEM education: within a decade, American students must 'move from the middle to the top of the pack in science and math.' Specifically, he [had] called on the nation to develop, recruit, and retain 100,000 excellent STEM teachers over the next 10 years. He also [had] asked colleges and universities to graduate an additional 1 million students with STEM majors. (Department of Education)

Although Barack Obama's actions have instrumentally paved the way for progress, it's now being inhibited in the most unexpected way. Given the current U.S. regime under President Donald J. Trump, such programs are likely to be forgotten or deprived. Trump's 2018 fiscal year budget cuts $776,000,000 from the National Science Foundation, which happens to be an 11% reduction. The Foundation is critically important as it grants funds for scientific research within STEM, and specifically engineering. Additionally, there's also a $1,000,000,000 cut to the National Cancer Institute, and an even greater $6,000,000,000 cut to the National Institute of Health. The United States may be home to Silicon Valley, the global capital of tech, but it is soon losing its superpower status in the field. When countries such as India and China are devoting a bountiful supply of resources to graduate more researchers, engineers, and computer scientists, we're losing a race that we never meant to concede. The scientific drive for discovery, ignited by Kennedy and the Apollo missions, is dying out. The fire is dying out, but we must stop it from dying forever. Therefore, it's imperative that we don't see these governmental roadblocks as impassable obstacles, but rather as temporary difficulties that pass and eventually give way to progress. The moment we start doubting the future is when we let the wall that limits us, envelop us.

Stanley Litow is the President of the IBM Foundation and is their Vice President of Corporate Citizenship & Corporate Affairs. In his article "A Silent Crisis: The Underrepresentation of Latinos in STEM", published in 2008, Litow detailed some of his worries about the lack of diversity in tech. Having been the deputy chancellor of New York City's schools, Litow believes STEM education is critically important to the future of America. He explains that the Department of Labor has projected a need for 50% more professionals with technological expertise in the near future, but we're simply not educating enough children. The problem isn't necessarily with our school system, but with the interests of our kids. Not enough minorities are choosing to pursue STEM, in contrast with their white and Asian peers. Hispanic men make up a very small percentage of the tech workforce The percentage of women is even smaller, at a nearly infinitesimal quantity. Litow persuades that what drives this country, and all countries, is innovation. And innovation is most efficiently driven by tech industries and pursuits — many of which are based in America. But there simply won't be enough engineers and computer scientists for us to keep advancing at the rate we need to, and the only way this problem can be fixed is if we graduate more students specializing in STEM. But we're not educating all the peoples we need to; we're not educating people from every economic class, ethnic background, race and gender. We're inadvertently concentrating our education on a few demographics, resulting in a stark selection bias. Litow furthers his thinking when he speaks of the Latino population, noting that, "American ingenuity, the foundation for our economic strength, has always been the product of our rich and diverse heritage" and that with "the country's growing Latino population, we have the classic paradox of challenge and opportunity."

As Litow explains, we simply need to be teaching more Hispanic children about the world of STEM. In very few cases are children simply not interested in tech pursuits. Rather, they're not even aware that they exist! This wall is what separates a better world from a partitioned one, and we need to move quick to tear it down. We need to start democratizing information about scientific careers, pursuits, and hobbies to inspire this nation's minority youth to get involved. Stressing the same idea, Litow writes that:

America's goal must be to raise the standard of living for all our children, not just some of them. To do this, we must take aggressive action. We must capture more minds and hearts, generate more passion for innovation...This is a moral imperative as well as an economic one. Whether one is in business, education, or community leadership, the time to join this effort is today. (Litow 2)

So, let's join that effort. Let's make a conscious effort to promote diversity and support programs, legislation or not, that advance our potential. Let's support our local neighborhoods in getting minority children interested in STEM. Let's donate our time and resources to make this a priority. Anyone can take these steps, whether you're a student, parent, or concerned citizen. After all, it's all up to you!

Currently, I live in the Southern California area, having moved from city to city every year since I turned four. I've been to all over the state, from San Francisco to Los Angeles, but I think it's accurate to say that I'm a SoCal native. My first neighborhood resided in the San Fernando Valley, where I made my first school friends and entered my first elementary school. Coincidentally, the Valley area is very Latino concentrated, so many of my first classmates and peers were Hispanic. I learned more and more about their culture, heritage, and tradition. For example, during show and tell and class parties, they would sometimes bring homemade food and describe it in detail. I was thoroughly fascinated — I was born in the U.S., but my family is originally from India. Before I'd landed in that school, I'd always be interacting with Indian family friends or distant cousins. That school may have just been a school, but to me it felt so much more than that.

Eventually, I moved to the East Bay area of San Francisco, and experienced a thoroughly different atmosphere. The Bay was a popular, suburban destination for families who worked in Silicon Valley: the tech capital of the world. It offered fantastic schools, a safe area, with community events and famous eateries. It was almost a picture perfect area — something that had been missing in the Valley. My school was mostly white and Asian, and it seemed as if everyone collectively held the same priorities: grades, test scores, and academic achievement. Additionally, there were very high standards being placed on the student body by the faculty and parents. This resulted in more funding, especially to the math and science department. The school encouraged more STEM programs, and even built a high school with a state of the art engineering academy. Students could choose to enroll at the beginning of freshman year and concentrate on STEM-oriented subjects, instead of following the traditional academic path. Some had even built programming portfolios by their sophomore year. I realized the stark differences between the two areas I had come from: the Valley, which had less funding and opportunity, and the Bay, which had breathtaking facilities specifically dedicated to the pursuit of science.

I realized at that moment the sheer privilege that had been afforded to me. Many of my peers on the East Bay had been born and raised there; to them, this was the world, and it was a bubble as well. It didn't occur to many of them that they were incredibly fortunate to have opportunities like these on hand. Back in the Valley, hundreds and hundreds of my peers would have been ecstatic to even visit the same facilities that the Bay had at hand. They would be overjoyed to participate in the STEM activities readily available, and their interests in science would skyrocket. It's just a matter of who happens to gain that privilege, and who doesn't — it's an opportunity gap.

If all children, Latino and all, were granted just as much funding and opportunity, we would definitely see an increase in STEM-matriculating college students. Again, the problem is rarely that kids are not interested in science — it's that many don't even know the applications it leads to. When many think of physics (even adults), they may think of complicated, long drawn equations, possibly reminiscent of a horrid teacher they once had in middle school. They don't think of the incredible technology that sends us racing to Mars, building our laptops, or engineering the printing presses this book is published from. When many think of programming, they might think of 17 year old nerds hard-coding these strange letters and numbers and symbols into a green screen, furiously, without taking a breath.

They don't think of the plethora of technologies we use in our day-to-day life that depend on code: phones, laptops, TVs, GPS, security systems, and even thermometers. When many think of mathematics, they might think of complex problems with enigmatic variables and lines. One of the lines from a math-hating friend that I find funny is, "I loved math until they started putting the letters into it. What was I supposed to do then?" Obviously, they were joking, but the ironic thing about it is mathematics, at its core, is very simple. Once you start to branch out, and learn more complex concepts, it might get more difficult. But it's crucial, vital, and central to the workings of our society, and it's essential that our children have a strong understanding of it.

So, I decided I wanted to try my hand at solving this problem. I'm fortunate to come from an area where opportunities are abundant and STEM education is top-notch. I decided that I was going to try to spread the wonder of STEM to those who might not be aware of it.

That's why I created She Dreams in Code. She Dreams in Code (SDIC) is a Southern California nonprofit dedicated to bringing awareness to the tech gender gap. Our goal is to increase STEM education in the inland empire of SoCal, as well as neighboring cities such as Santa Ana and Costa Mesa. By targeting areas that are Hispanic-concentrated, we're ensuring that we try to spread the wonder of STEM to an underrepresented minority. SDIC intends to advocate for related counties to adopt more science curriculum and provide further ventures for interested students to take up. Unlike the Bay, many of these areas might have difficulty enrolling and preparing for events such as the Science Fair, which are often the first encounters STEM-bound students have with organized competitions. Additionally, programs such as Lego and FIRST robotics are disproportionately available to wealthier communities. SDIC aims to contact school boards and heads of departments to discuss more STEM pursuits with the student body. Hopefully, new programs will be implemented and more Latino students will choose STEM when matriculating into college or selecting a career. Either way, we'll be adequately preparing our children for the next chapter of the world — the tech revolution.

It's the era that changes everything. Many jobs will be automated to reduce costs, and many careers we'd never even imagined before will have been created. For example, twenty years ago, who would've thought we'd have an official occupation titled 'app developer'? More and more new technologies will be developed, and the tech revolution is going to produce one of the largest opportunity gaps in our history: the 'haves' with adequate STEM skills and the 'have nots' with none. We need to make sure our children are on the winning side. That's why STEM programs are so important and that's exactly what SDIC aims to promote. Technological careers are incredibly lucrative. The Economics and Statistics

Administration of the U.S. Department of Commerce released a study titled *STEM: Good Jobs Now and for the Future.* Within it, they described the various benefits of training America to pursue more tech occupations. Backed up with accurate research, the Administration claimed that "STEM workers command higher wages, earning 26 percent more than their non-STEM counterparts" and that "[on] average, [STEM workers] earned almost $25 per hour, $9 more per hour than those in other occupations in 2010."

Let's do some quick math (I know, it's a good thing!). Let's say Employee #1 works in a STEM-affiliated occupation, and Employee #2 does not. Employee #1, therefore, earns about $25 an hour, while Employee #2 earns about $16 — both respectable wages. But let's see how this plays out long term. Let's take a look at Employee #1's typical set-up:

- $25/hr
- 8 hr/day
- 5 days/week
- 50 weeks/year

Let's look at Employee #2:
- $16/hr
- 10hr/day (note that this is 2 hours more than Employee #1 spends working)
- 5 days/week

- 50 weeks/year

Now, let's get into the math by starting with Employee #1:

(\$25 hr/day) x (8 hr/day) x (5 days/week) x (50 weeks/year)

$$= \$50,000$$

And the math for Employee #2:

(\$16 hr/day) x (10 hr/day) x (5 days/week) x (50 weeks/year)

$$= \$40,000$$

That's a big difference. Despite working two hours more per day, the non-STEM worker earns \$10,000 less than the STEM-worker, and that's 25% of their total salary! If we work to equalize the amount of the hours, the difference would be even larger. The benefits of pursuing STEM far outweigh the costs, even when you include undergraduate tuition and college expenses. That's why SDIC believes that it's absolutely imperative that we're encouraging our children to pursue STEM, because there's a financial consequence to not doing so.

Nelson Mandela was a famed revolutionary who helped eradicate apartheid in South Africa. On grounds of race, dark-skinned citizens of the nation were often limited by the enforced racial segregation. Mandela, steady in his belief that knowledge is what breaks chains, once said that "education is the most powerful tool you can use to change the world." And it's true: education is the path to freedom. Schooling, literacy, and academia are all fantastic sources of knowledge and thinking.

But right now, many minority children aren't receiving their equal share of quality STEM education. And because of this, they're simply not aware of the opportunities that lie before them — the opportunities that will vanish very quickly. We're at a unique point in time where technological and coding skills are niche. Most people know how to operate a computer or digital device, but many have no idea how it works. But in twenty, thirty, forty years, basic coding skills will be as common as reading. And what's even more fascinating is that this has been seen before in the profession of the typist. Typists were commonly hired to type various documents, letters, and notes using a typewriter or a computer device. Many typists were active in the '60s and '70s, but just as the new millennium rolled around, the job was basically nonexistent. Nearly everyone in the first world had now become capable of efficiently typing for themselves. And coding will eventually be the same — we might not all be master programmers, but the average person will definitely know more than they might today.

It's all a matter of perspective and prediction. We need to prepare our children to beat the curve instead of being enveloped by it. All the tell-tale signs of a social and economic revolution are coming — it's up to us to make sure our youth are capable, technologically. And we can even start now. STEM-based careers are lucrative and stable — let's help our poorest children by motivating them to pursue the sciences. That way, we are able to ensure financial security and a valuable contribution to society.

So what SDIC plans to do is ignite that spark. All of us already have the infrastructure around us: schools, libraries, youth organizations, and afterschool centers. Let's focus on turning those into STEM hubs, so any child interested can have access to fun and encouraging scientific activities. At its core, SDIC is a 'helping hand' organization. If we see a program that desperately needs funding, perhaps a robotics class in Santa Ana that's member-less, we're going to try our best to ensure their success. We'll do this by fundraising, spreading awareness, and personally advocating around the area to make the biggest difference. Reaching out to prominent tech companies asking for grants and capital is not out of the question either. We also intend to introduce new educational opportunities and possible curriculum that could be used to deliver important concepts. SDIC plans to visit and speak to several regional school boards to cooperate to come to a solution for our children: a solution that values a concentration of STEM education in the areas that need it most.

But often, a child may not be interested in becoming an engineer or a computer scientist. Their passion may be in law, and they may be eager to pursue politics as a career. And that's totally fine! Our world is made up of billions of unique people, each with their own desires and aspirations. What is important, however, is that these children are aware of the promising technological applications that can come with areas associated with the liberal arts. For example, there's 'hard STEM' pursuits — careers that are heavily focused on the principles of science, technology, engineering, and math. These could be occupations such as aerospace engineering, software development, and bioinformatics. Often, this is what many associate STEM with when they hear the term. But there's so much more: there's the 'soft STEM' pursuits. Soft STEM careers are careers which can intertwine technological applications and a non-technical occupation. For instance, this could be a business executive in a tech company, a tech-specific lawyer, or a journalist who specializes in the tech field. In my opinion, jobs that combine the humanity of liberal arts and the efficiency of technology are the most valuable, as being able to communicate and create is a golden combination.

I'm fascinated with the applications of artificial intelligence. Many, when they think of AI, think of malicious robots or vengeful humanoids. And although both those combinations can be true, thankfully they're not! AI isn't just limited to movie magic, and it's actually doing things we never thought capable. For example, recently, the Japanese novel *Konpyuta ga shosetsu wo kaku hi*, or *The Day a Computer Writes a*

Novel was autonomously written by an AI program. An entire novel! And what's even more captivating is that it almost won one of the most prestigious Japanese literary awards.

Another facet of AI that is evolving is the concept of 'Deep Writing'. The website, run by editor Max Deutsch and writer Lalith Polepeddi, offers a fantastic array of actual pieces written by AI programs. Basically, once you feed a sample of text, the computer analyzes it and, using a complex program, can assemble its own version of the story. Cool, right?

It's this intersection between the liberal arts and new technology that is truly going to be valuable. So how does SDIC intend to spread this message to those who may be uninformed?

Well, we're first going to try to establish ourselves as a known technological nonprofit in SoCal. By making our presence known, we're simultaneously promoting the cause. Secondly, in order to support tech initiatives in the area, we're going to seek out grants and funds from major companies. Google, Facebook, and Apple have all acknowledged the gender gap and are proactively trying to close it. We will also aim to connect with top tech leaders in the field to raise awareness, capital, and cooperative efforts.

The gender gap is a global problem. It might seem that because Silicon Valley, and tech itself, is clustered in the U.S., that the issue only exists within North America. The fact is that the increasing of STEM education is not just a domestic problem but international as well. The ultimate goal, in fact, should be to educate the world's citizens; not just America's.

For instance, the United Kingdom has also taken notice of its own gender diversity issue. CA Technologies, a company that operates internationally, has written about how children's study choices in schooling affect the overall diversity of technology. They note that "just 7% of girls move into higher STEM programmes against 24% of boys on the same path." They also noted the stark choices when it came to more advanced educational options. For those unaware, the A-levels are roughly the U.K. equivalent of AP classes in the United States. They're advanced classes specializing in a subject, and they often follow GCSEs (General Certificate of Secondary Education). A-levels are available in a wide range of subjects such as classical languages, physics, English literature, mathematics, and geography. The company wrote that "when it came to moving on to A-Levels, Advanced Apprenticeships or Level 3 Vocational Qualifications, there were 237,509 boys and 97,557 girls." What's even more alarming? 66% of girls opt out of any and all STEM courses at this stage. That means only 34% of all girls take even one STEM course!

The organization techUK is the representative for the United Kingdom technological scene. Even Jacqueline de Rojas, the current president of techUK, has commented on these discrepancies, claiming "girls taking computing at A Level has declined by 70% — and boys are four times more likely to take IT GCSE than girls." It's almost an exact copy of America's AP Computer Science problem — not enough girls are choosing to take programming courses. And in the U.K., where the A-levels you take could potentially determine your career, it's especially important. If you don't take the specific A-levels required, you might not be able to earn a degree in computer science. And that's bad news for the diversification problem in Great Britain, because if girls tentatively opt out due to temporary peer pressure, that may affect them for years to come.

That's why the WISE campaign, based in Britain, has dedicated itself to encouraging more girls to stick with STEM subjects, like physics and computing. Their mission is simple: tackle the gender gap from, as they say, classroom to boardroom. Similar to many American organizations, they believe the only way to true equality is equality at the top of the ladder and at the bottom. As a result, they encourage more and more female leaders, while motivating young girls all around the U.K. to persevere through hardship. In fact, they even offer specialized resources to various schools and companies to correct the disparities.

But perhaps their greatest achievement has been their People Like Me campaign. Often, girls choose not to pursue STEM as a result of being the 'outsider'. The most harmful yet frequent phrase is that tech careers aren't for "people like me". In essence, it's a euphemism for being different, even though that difference shouldn't matter. But the United Kingdom is in a dire situation right now, just as the U.S. is. For example they're only graduating a fraction of the STEM workers they need. At this time, the majority of graduating engineers and computer scientists are overwhelmingly from India and China. As a result, we're not seeing a domestic cultivation of innovation in either America or Great Britain. And the structuring of the British education system makes this even worse, as there's generally very little flexibility involved. Recently, according to WISE, out of an astounding 14,000 engineering apprentices, just 450 were girls. My math tells me that's approximately 3.21%, which is shocking. In a country that is 50% female, only 3.21% of their engineering apprentices are female! That's only 3 out of every 100! And this can all be attributed to that one short, succinct, and damaging phrase: "I thought about it, but you know — it's not really for people like me."

So WISE decided to change the perspective of the British youth with a revolutionary new program. The People Like Me campaign launched in 2015, and it's been an apparent success. In essence, according to the organization itself, "People Like Me is a revolutionary approach to engaging girls with careers in Science, Technology, Engineering and Maths (STEM). People Like Me uses the natural tendency of girls to articulate their self-identity using adjectives, to show them that people like them are happy and successful working in careers in

STEM." Basically, WISE is using smart word-association to persuade young girls that they are capable of pursuing these fields, and that their gender is neither a disadvantage nor an impediment. It acts as a case study of sorts – it presents the young girls with role models — women in the field who are satisfied, fulfilled, and having fun in their respective careers. Seeing 'people like you' who are going against the grain *and* feel accepted is a powerful thing, and the app has been downloaded many times. Additionally, they offer informational sessions, training to teach the program, and schooling resources. It's wrapped up into a nice, little package that has a remarkable effect on the views of young girls.

My personal favorite part of the campaign is the 12 Types of Scientist aptitude test. Participating girls are given a sheet with various adjectives labelled, including "inventive", "persistent", "friendly", "artistic", "persuasive", and "helpful". Whichever words they most identify with, they check off and, at the end, all the checkmarks are counted in their respective boxes. The program also provides a handy key in order to see what type of scientist you are, depending on what adjectives you chose!

There are 12 different types of scientist you can receive: Explorer, Investigator, Developer, Service Provider, Regulator, Entrepreneur, Communicator, Trainer, Persuader, Supporter, Manager, and Policy maker. All the titles have different characteristics associated with them, but they all imply a sense of belonging within technology — they're all advocating for more female engineers.

The Explorer is pragmatic and curious. She's always trying to figure out why things work the way to do, and she's absolutely fascinated with science and its applications. Although she likes working alone, she's open to collaborating with others and loves to hear what they think. In her free time, she likes experimenting on any ideas she has, and she's always up to solve a really challenging puzzle. She's inquisitive and loves figuring things out. WISE recommends that girls who identify as Explorers look into careers such as being a Professor, Pharmacist, Geneticist, Test Engineer, and Astronomer.

The Investigator is great at working in a group. Unlike the Explorer, which may like to figure things out before everyone else, the Investigator takes a more collaborative approach when solving a problem. Everything she does in the scientific realm is calm, cool, and collected — she's very logical and organized. She's almost a detective of sorts, as she loves to find out small bits of information and eventually piece together the entire mystery. She likes working and chatting with other people, and tries to be helpful when she can. WISE recommends that girls who identify as investigators consider working in the R&D (research and development) sectors of businesses and universities in order to fully take advantage of their methodical thought process.

The Developer is concerned with cooperation and creation. They absolutely love to sit down with an idea and, somehow, make it happen. They're endlessly creative, artistic, and practical. Generally, they're excellent at design, and if working for a particular agency or client, their communication skills are sure to get the job done. They want to advance the world with their work, and they're constantly looking at the bigger picture. Their capacity to sympathize and empathize distinguishes them from the other types. WISE proposes that Developers pursue careers that have them building their own creations, under businesses, universities, or a third party agency.

Being one of the most 'people-friendly' types, the Service Provider always serves with a smile. She's respectful and gracious, while entertaining great communication skills. She's a bridge between the highly technical realm and the rest of the world. A Service Provider is more than capable of getting a message across, especially to people who may not have a large technical vocabulary. Meticulous, the Service Provider is a near perfectionist, and loves condensing information into simple-to-understand bits. WISE suggests Service Providers check out governmental professions central to technology, as their communication skills are key in passing the STEM-specific legislation at the right magnitude and time.

The Regulator is constantly on the watch for disaster — she's a superhero of sorts! As a scientist, she's concerned with the finer details that others might overlook. She has a very strong sense of self and sense of justice. She knows that the power of science can often be the difference between life and death, so she's committed to making everything as safe as possible. The Regulator is honest, objective, and law-abiding — but she's not afraid to stand up for what's right. She's always looking out for the public, and if something isn't up to standards, she's more than ready to scrap the idea. WISE recommends that Regulators work in independent laboratories that check products on the market for safety and legitimacy.

A fledgling innovator, the Entrepreneur is eager to socialize and sell. Charismatic and brilliant, they're often the ones who take charge and direct their vision exactly the way they want it. They know how to interact with people, know what motivates people, and most importantly, know how to cooperate and compromise with them. She is creative and focused — they're dedicated to serving the customer and they want to make sure their experience is as smooth as it can be. The Entrepreneur is a born leader, taking charge when necessary while allowing efficient teamwork to occur. The WISE campaign suggests that Entrepreneurs seek out occupations such as Business Analyst, Chief Executive Officer, Founding Director, and of course, entrepreneurship as well.

If we lived in a TV-centric world, the Communicator would be your favorite news anchor. She's talented in breaking down critical pieces of information into easy-to-understand messages, all while keeping it interesting. The Communicator is very familiar with the channels of social media and how to communicate effectively with others. Along with the Service Provider, she is natural with people and loves to have a productive conversation. WISE recommends Communicators seek out careers that allow them to interact over different media, including radio, TV, and advertising.

The Trainer is your best friend who's incredibly smart, but kind as well. She loves to help others when she can, and feels especially proud when she can make a real difference. She's incredibly knowledgeable, while using her intelligence for all the right reasons. The Trainer may love to be the center of attention, but that's because she enjoys sharing what she knows with the world. WISE lists potential careers for Trainers to be teaching, journalism, museum curator, and science communicator.

Armed with sweet talking and captivation, the Persuader can change your opinion on nearly anything. They're organized and ready for anything, all while keeping a cool head under pressure. They excel under pressure, and are able to meet set deadlines with ease. A Persuader is creative, a designer, and enjoys talking with other people. WISE suggests careers in advertising and marketing for potential Persuaders in order to fully utilize that charismatic magic.

The Supporter is pivotal to the livelihood of any major organization. Communication is key to them, and they enjoy interacting with other people, outside and inside work environments. They're eager to help in any way they can, exceeding expectations in nearly everything they may do for a client. Their aim is to constantly keep improving themselves and the world around them, all while keeping a smile on their faces. Supporters make friends easily, and they can make small talk with nearly everyone. WISE recommends that Supporters consider careers in customer relations within various corporations.

Managers are dedicated to a plan. They strike the perfect balance between organization and improvisation, always knowing what to do when the time comes. Their main goal is efficiency, and they try their best to achieve the best results possible. They strive for the absolute best, all while aptly coordinating with a team or crew. Managers can work with other people and inspire them to develop the best things they could possibly create. Potential careers for Managers might include working in businesses of various sizes and as consultants of sorts.

The Policy Maker wants to change the world. They want to directly influence the course of legislation by getting involved with politics and government. They tend to encourage a collaborative spirit, but are not afraid of influencing the status quo. Policy Makers tend to enjoy working in local and national governments. They may also act as advisors to voted representatives in order to influence certain legislation.

WISE has certainly established themselves in the U.K. and are using their influence to provide fantastic resources to young girls. Remember, in order to tackle the issue of the gender gap, there are 3 steps: change, cooperation, and commemoration. WISE is excelling at changing the biases of young girls, cooperating with local and regional communities, and commemorating successful women in tech to their audience.

Something that we all, with hope, will encourage today and tomorrow.

I was born and raised in Southern California, but my family is originally from India. Home to more than 1.3 billion individuals, it is soon expected to pass China as the most populous nation in the world. India is home to a diverse and rich variety of cultures, languages, and traditions, many of them distinct and unique. Occasionally, we try to visit during our summers, traveling around the southern tip of the country. A couple years ago, we visited the city of Chennai, the hometown of both my mother and father. We decided to rent out a hotel in a nice suburb near the urban area, to ensure that we'd have a quality stay while being close to the main action. We checked into a rather quaint inn, with traditional Indian ornaments and novelties. Statuettes of the Hindu gods decorated the room, each one crafted with meticulous carvings and artistry. We settled within a room on the ground floor, and then proceeded to organize our things into the various cabinets and shelves. A few hours later, we heard a knock on our door – it was the maid. In India, maids are often hired individually, and not necessarily by a particular company or organization. Therefore, many young women in the country take up the occupation, as it's an accessible way of making some money.

This woman looked to be in her late thirties, and although she was relatively young, she seemed to be sprouting gray hairs and worn wrinkles. She wasn't like the many maids I had met in the States; she was very personable and struck up conversations as she was cleaning. The first time she saw us, she asked us who we were, where we came from, and why we came to visit. The second time she saw us, we had a lengthy conversation on what is was like in America versus the town of Madurai, where she was from. She had never been outside of Tamil Nadu — the state we were in — and, like most of her family, had longed to visit the States. In India, America is viewed as a golden opportunity: it's the promised land of sorts, and anyone who manages to become a citizen and settle in the country is treated with great respect. The woman, who I will call Revathi, was very interested in our lives in California. We took a great liking to her, and eventually she would pop up by our door every day for a ten minute chat.

After a little over a week, we realized that although we'd told her a great deal about us, we knew very little about her. All we knew was that her name was Revathi, she worked in a small inn near Chennai, and she was from Madurai originally. On the other hand, she now knew where we went to school, when we arrived in America, where we were from in India, where we planned to visit, why we wanted to visit, and knew about our family here in Chennai. So, we decided to reciprocate and ask her a little more about herself.

So, the next day, when we focused the conversation on her, Revathi was very surprised at first; she told us that not many people ever ask her about her life. She initially didn't know what to say, but given a minute or so, she was soon divulging her entire life story.

One thing that caught my ear was her family. She described that she had two children: a boy of about seventeen, and a girl of about eleven. Although they were very bright, she said, they were not at all motivated to complete their schooling. In India, and similar countries, schooling isn't required by law under the government. That means if you decided not to formally educate your son or daughter, you would have no problem legally. America, however, is a different story.

When I later asked my mother about this, she responded that although it wasn't very common in urban areas, in rural areas choosing not to educate your children was common. The reason for this was pure, temporary practicality. Many of those who live in rural areas in India are farmers — and farmers, undeniably, need labor. Often, people will choose not to enroll their sons or daughters in school as, in their mind, time spent at school is time wasted, which could be better used working at home.

Revathi continued. Now fairly invested in the conversation, she meticulously detailed how difficult it was to manage her son and daughter with little to no money, at just twenty-three. Her husband had died that year, and it seemed as if she was all alone, with no family or friends to support her. Her mother had been a maid at a hotel, and occasionally cleaned people's homes to supplement her income. Revathi decided that she could not sit idly when she could provide her children with a better life. She decided, at that time, to be a maid. She would often bring her children with her to work, managing them and carrying out her duties at the same time. She faced much scrutiny, with many assuming that she was an unwed teenager, unworthy of their respect. But she deserved more respect than anyone: managing two children at such a young age is surely a respectable thing.

Once Revathi turned thirty, things started looking up. She was able to build her income up to a healthy amount, and she and her children could enjoy life as it came. But she would always tell them one thing, every night, and every morning, before they went to school and after they came back: always, always aim higher. Revathi's mother had been a cleaner, and her mother had been a cleaner, and her mother had been a cleaner — so on and so forth. It was almost a family tradition. Her mother, like her own mother, had kept Revathi from school when she was young in order to help her clean. Every day, instead of learning basic arithmetic and spelling, Revathi would be cleaning alongside her mother, house by house, day by day. And eventually, many of Revathi's friends immigrated to the U.S., U.K, and Canada in search of a better and more prosperous life. Revathi, however, was constrained. It was then that she realized the power of education: the power of words, literacy, and learning. She realized that no matter how hard she tried, it would be almost impossible to escape, once and for all, the 100-mile radius that limited her and her children. And it all came down to one thing: education.

Revathi told us that she didn't give her children much of a choice. After her children came home, she said, you either reviewed today's material or studied for tomorrow's. You didn't go out with friends every weekend; instead, you studied for next week's examinations. You didn't aim for passing; you aimed for first rank.

Revathi instilled in her children an unparalleled drive and passion. They might not have had all the fun in the world, but they sure had a much more promising future. At the time we met her, Revathi was proud to tell us that her son had recently been accepted into a prestigious engineering school and was planning on attending. Her daughter had similar goals in mind.

It is easy to simply wish for a solution for world hunger and poverty. But instead of trying to create one, let's focus our efforts on something that we know, for certain, will break the chains of hardship and will instill hope of prosperity. Revathi's story not only confirms but encourages this way of thinking. Let's stop trying to fix something that isn't broken, and instead focus on improving what we're already aware of: the power of education.

In this scheme of things, issues are rarely as simple as black and white. It would be wrong to assume that the most urgent, educational-based problem that our world faces today is STEM education. Even though it is incredibly important, it's not the most pressing matter at the moment. First world countries like Britain and the U.S. are taking active steps to close the gap, but in countries where girls are not even allowed to partake in basic schooling, there is much more work to be done before we can achieve equality. We need to democratize any and all educational resources before we devote all our time and energy into STEM-specific matters.

Somalia is a coastal country that lies on the Eastern shore of Africa. Home to more than 14,000,000 people, its inhabitants have suffered tremendously due to violent and continuous civil war. The nation is in total disarray, and is considered by many to be one of the most underdeveloped countries in the world. Unfortunately, someone has to pay the price for all the conflict and disorder that occurs on a daily bases. As in most conflicts, children are the ones who suffer dearly. Due to the constant chaos and brutality, the Somali youth have lost their right to a proper, formal, and safe education. But perhaps the most affected are young girls. Nearly every society, since the dawn of human civilization, has put an increased value on a son's education versus a daughter's. When times were tough and money was scarce, many families actively chose to pay their son's tuition instead of their daughter's — you couldn't do both, so you had to choose. It didn't matter how much promise you had or how much passion you had for learning. You were automatically denied the most important things in this world: literacy and education. From there, it's a downward slope. It's very hard to escape the cycles of poverty without a proper education. Knowing how to read, write, and do basic math is pivotal in helping you survive in the modern world. If one has lost the opportunity for education, the chance of a better life is nearly zero. It's unfortunately commonplace in third-world countries like Somalia, and the situation needs our help to change.

The organization UNICEF (the United Nations Children's Fund) frequently aids underdeveloped countries in educational and medical needs, often coming to the aid of mothers and their children. A platform of the peacekeeping United Nations, their mission is to defend the rights of every child, globally. Right now, they're pouring time, energy, and resources into helping any youth they can find in the battle-stricken regions of Somalia.

UNICEF agrees that the educational status in Somalia is in dire times. Very few children actually seem to be enrolled in schools. In fact, only 40% are, and out of that 40%, a massive 70% are boys. In stark contrast, in the States it's illegal to withhold any child from schooling, and it can actually be punishable by jail time. According to the National Center for Education Statistics, in 2014, a whopping 98% of 7 to 13 year olds were enrolled in either public or private schools. In the States, there are actually millions more females enrolling in college programs than males.

But Somalia is a different story. A country scarred by war, its inhabitants are afraid of sending their girls to school. According to UNICEF in their article *Education in Somalia*, "Girls' participation in education is consistently lower than that for boys. Fewer than 50 percent of girls attend primary school, and....only 25 percent of women aged 15 to 24 were literate."

Literacy, in the modern world, is the first step towards breaking the wheel of poverty. For generations, it can spin over and over and over again. But the moment a woman is able to learn, to read, to write, the wheel can be destroyed. It is entirely possible that every cycle of poverty can be cured by a quality education. But the young girls of Somalia don't receive anything close to that. In fact, the "low availability of sanitation facilities (especially separate latrines for girls), a lack of female teachers

…safety concerns and social norms that favour boys' education are cited as factors inhibiting parents from enrolling their daughters in school." The system, in many ways, overwhelmingly favors males as the cultural norm. We've talked about how the media can shape our views of gender over long periods of time. Well, Somalia, and similar countries, exemplify the consequences of this on a mass scale. There is hardly any equality in the world these young girls live in. The schools they attend cannot sanitarily accommodate them, their safety is risked every time they step out the door, and they're constantly devalued at every turn in their lives. How are we going to make a difference in their world if we're not actively reaching out to them, telling them they're worth it, making sure they know that they're special, unique, and intelligent? For those of us living fairly comfortably in the first-world, we cannot turn a blind eye to those overseas. Often, we become numb to the struggles of others, and after a while, it seems less and less important to us. We can't allow that to happen anymore — our collective detachment is indirectly responsible for the plight of these girls. If we, as a community, as a state, as a nation, and as a world make an active effort to cooperate with each other rather than playing a game of politics and cunning, we might just change everything.

But this isn't just happening in Somalia, or other African countries. It's happening in many parts of the globe, especially in the Asian continent. Let's take Myanmar, also known as Burma, a country located in Southeast Asia. It's home to nearly 53,000,000 people, and the nation itself borders Laos, Thailand, India, Bangladesh, and China. Unfortunately, it's also wrapped up in one of the longest civil wars in the world – various Burmese ethnic groups are constantly at war with one another, and the result is a nation with a system of human rights violations. Myanmar has frequently been documented by the United Nations as being a source of numerous civil transgressions.

UNESCO (the United Nations Educational, Scientific and Cultural Organization) has been documenting gender struggles in Myanmar for a long time now. According to UNESCO, their goal as a peacemaking organization is to make sure every child is equipped with a quality education in a safe environment. When studying Myanmar, UNESCO made the decision to interview the young boys of the villages most affected by gender inequality. What they found was astounding and a genuine display of human empathy,

UNESCO Bangkok traveled to these regions of Myanmar and asked male schoolchildren about their younger, illiterate sisters. One boy in particular, Yan, became very emotional as he was approached. According to UNESCO's article, *Myanmar's gender challenges in education: What the boys have to say*, "[when] asked about his older sister, Yan cannot hold back his tears. The 13-year-old student recalls how his sister dropped out of… at age 10. Since then she has been selling fish to help her dad... support her brother's education." Stories like these are far from uncommon in Myanmar. It's a familiar tale: a family is born with a son, and they're delighted — it's just what they were hoping for. They pray for their next one to be another boy, and are thoroughly disappointed when they see a daughter in front of them. And if more daughters appear, it seems as if their lives are ruined. After all, where will the family name go? Where will be the breadwinners? When might we marry them off?

This isn't hyperbole. In countries like Myanmar, it's second nature to value your son's education over your daughter's. It's obvious to them. We might see it as appalling; after all, you're making a child work long hours and days to support their older brother's education, without basic respect and appreciation. But to the citizens of similar countries, this is their way of life. It doesn't matter if women in the first world have won the right to vote, be elected by the populace, and govern from the highest chair of the land. This is how it's always been, so it's 'how it will always be'. There is no room for change. There is no room for progress. There is only room for what has been and what is expected to continue.

UNESCO documents their further findings in the article. Commenting on the prevailing nature of gender inequality, they state:

[Tales like Yan's are] all too common in Myanmar, where attaining education is a difficult feat for many females despite it being constitutionally guaranteed for all. While most girls attend primary school, the numbers gradually decrease at the secondary and higher education levels. In 2015, more than 1.7 million women over 15 in Myanmar were found to be illiterate...according to the UNESCO Institute for Statistics. (UNESCO)

Such events are common in South Asia as well. Pakistan, a country with over 200,000,000 people, borders India, Afghanistan, and Iran. It's the seventh most populous nation in the world. But in 1970, there were approximately 112 males born for every 100 females, which is an alarming instance of disproportionality. This number has decreased to 105 in 2015, but it's still not as equal as countries like the U.S. and Great Britain. The lack of women, or more precisely, the lack of female children, is partly due to societal norms and conventions within Pakistan. Sons are a golden achievement, while daughters are looked at as a burden. As a result, fewer and fewer citizens are opting to have children if they are predicted to be daughters. It's appalling, startling, and concerning, but unfortunately, very real.

As you can imagine, this mentality plays into education as well. UNESCO, in their October 2012 paper *Education For All Global Monitoring Report*, centered on the education system in

Pakistan. UNESCO revealed that "Pakistan has the world's second highest number of children out of school, reaching 5.1 million in 2010." A country that makes up less than 3% of the global population constitutes over 8% of children out of school — a remarkably disproportionate ratio. In a world where proper education is absolutely critical in escaping cycles of poverty, Pakistan is inadequately preparing their youth for the new age to come.

But that's not the worst of it. The Pakistani Taliban, a reprehensible terrorist organization, has regularly been trying to curb the gender equality movement in Pakistan. For years, many female advocates have been fighting for the right to a formal education, which is banned for many girls in Taliban controlled areas. Their presence has definitely made a mark on the overall dynamics of gender in schooling; according to UNESCO, "two-thirds of Pakistan's out of school children are girls, amounting to over 3 million girls out of school." But their mission is to control the one thing that can grant freedom upon these girls, and that's education. As the saying goes, a simple pen and simple word can win the war without lifting a sword. Unfortunately, the Taliban still takes violent measures to ensure that young girls are not taught to read or write. They have not been above bombing and terrorizing schools and advocacy organizations for their causes.

But one teenager was courageous enough to stand up to them. Malala Yousafzai, born on July 12, 1997, was raised in the

Swat Valley of Pakistan. Her father had been involved in humanitarian work, and her family ran a chain of schools around the vicinity educating local children. It was here that Yousafzai discovered the power of literacy and knowledge, and the downfalls that can come without it. Without formal education, it is often difficult to separate propaganda from facts, and blissful lies from truth. A lack of schooling makes it easier for someone to shape your opinions for you, and this was exactly what the Taliban intended to do.

So, starting in 2009, Yousafzai began to write an anonymous blog for BBC Urdu, detailing life under Taliban rule. Just eleven or twelve years of age, she had discovered her passion for equal education and human rights. Shortly after, the New York Times created a documentary describing her life, and she quickly became a symbol for hope in a region of such devastation.

This all changed with the click of a trigger. On the afternoon of October 9th, 2012, a Taliban gunman entered Yousafzai's school bus in an effort to assassinate her. To them, she was a symbol of peace, hope, and equality — everything that threatened their agenda.. Yousafzai sustained a bullet to the face, and was immediately placed in intensive care and eventually flown to the U.K. for treatment. The Taliban intended to do what they do often: use their intimidation tactics and fear-mongering to frighten those who would dare for a better life. But instead of putting out the fire, they had only lit the spark.

Immediately, Yousafzai became an international icon for the struggles of young girls everywhere. Miraculously recovering, she soon went on to create The Malala Fund, a nonprofit dedicated to educational equality for women everywhere. She co-authored the bestselling title *I Am Malala: The Story of the Girl Who Stood Up for Education and Was Shot by the Taliban*, a book detailing her journey as a girl from the Swat Valley to being an international symbol. Within *Malala*, she described the importance of advocacy and human rights, going so far as to say that "We realize the importance of our voices only when we are silenced." In 2014, she received the Nobel Peace Prize for her efforts and courage in the field of education, becoming the youngest-ever recipient of the award.

What Malala shows us is that anyone can be a hero. We might think of heroes as masked men and women in capes, with superpowers and exotic backstories. But the truth is, heroes surround us every day, and not necessarily in capes or colored masks. Some may greet you with medical scrubs, a lab coat, a helping hand, a warm smile. Anyone can be a hero, and even if you're a 17 year old girl, you can do incredible things. Yousafzai has overcome a myriad of obstacles to get to where she is, and she continues to push for all those still suffering under unjust oppression and tyranny.

It's the responsibility of every capable person to advocate to close this educational gap. This isn't something particular to one area or group of people: as we've seen, it's prevalent in three distinct regions thousands of miles apart. Each of them have their own cultures, religions, and languages, but they still struggle in systemic ways to promote simple equality. It's a very complex matter and can be attributed to many different issues. The key thing to understand is that we can't simply ignore this. The active support of first world powers and global organizations like the United Nations, and active cooperation from countries with extreme gender gaps in education and literacy, are both pivotal to progress. Collaboration is the only way to move forward — this can't be achieved by any one person or country. But each of us can choose to do our part: to volunteer, to donate, to spread awareness.

The core of this problem isn't economic or political, although it certainly could be used to further certain agendas. This is a moral issue that envelops millions of young students every day. We may not see them, or hear from them, or even know of them — but they're there, and it would be wrong to ignore their plight when we have the resources and ability to help. And this isn't a zero-sum game: good things will happen for everyone if we, collectively, choose to make an active effort in closing the educational gap.

UNESCO, in their October 2013 report *Girls' Education*, brought to light many truths of women in the developing worlds. Often, it is asked what is the benefit of providing more and more capital and resources to further causes such as these. We've seen how this affects the tech community, and how having more diversity means more innovation. But when it comes to general education, what's the benefit of spending money and time in remedying this gap? UNESCO aimed to answer these exact questions. Apart from doing a moral service, the organization provided other, surprising incentives for increasing education access for young girls. Outlined here in a few points, UNESCO stated that:

- "If all mothers completed primary education, maternal deaths would be reduced by two-thirds, saving 98,000 lives."
- "If all women had a secondary education, child deaths would be cut in half, saving 3 million lives."
- "If all women had a secondary education, 12 million children would be saved from stunting from malnutrition."
- "If all girls had a secondary education, there would be two-thirds fewer child marriages."
- "Girls and young women who are educated have greater awareness of their rights, and greater confidence and freedom to make decisions that affect their lives."

Tech is encompassing. Increasing opportunities for these girls, by not only providing primary and secondary education but also advancing STEM education, is the way to solve the world's problems. Name any threat that our world faces today, natural or manmade: the reality is that 99% of these scenarios can be remedied with proper cooperation with others and the utilization of technological resources. We live in a world where we can create anything, so instead of developing more and more problems, let's invent more solutions.

What we need is more engineers, more creators, and more thinkers. We need people who are passionate, brave, and ready to take on the world. We need more solutions, and people who will be hungry to delve into those solutions. Tech will take over our world, and it'll continue at nearly the same pace as it's doing right now. But years from now, we'll realize just how far we've come. And in order for us to look upon that moment with pride, we need to make sure we're encouraging the right things, starting with 'tech feminism': the intellectual equality of men and women, of all races, in the STEM sector. And perhaps, one day, girls and boys everywhere will see gender bias as a thing of the past, forgotten, and never present.

A NEW GENERATION OF GIRLS

We've come a long way from where we were. It hasn't even been a hundred years since we've been granted the right to vote, and we're already making our mark on politics and the government. Fifty years ago, it would have been strange to see a woman pursuing graduate degrees in math or science. Now, no one bats an eye. But even with all this progress, there's no doubt that we still have more to do. We've only paved a section of the road, but there's still miles ahead of us. The girls of today all have something to owe to the pioneers of the past: they made female leadership normal.

It might be easy to get discouraged at all the obstacles in your way. It might be easy to ignore the problem. It might be easy to pretend that it's unsolvable, and choose to live with the circumstances. But you see, the young girls of today form a new generation of girls — a generation of girls who grew up in the information age, with access to strong female role models in the media or elsewhere if they looked. They are aware of the problems they face, but they come eager to brainstorm solutions. They're not the type to back down from a conflict, or provoke it: they're the ones who will remedy it. This new generation of girls is going to do something no other generation has ever done: make incredible strides to close the gender gap and limit bias in the tech world.

We've grown up with Instagram, Snapchat, and Twitter. We've never known a life without the internet, and smartphones have always been the norm. We can't believe there was a time where people couldn't walk around with a wireless phone, or that there were these strange items called pagers. We've been the main consumer market for social media and digital technology – so now, it's time to be the ones creating them. We know what users want, because we're active users ourselves. We have more power than most demographics in America. Young women can make or break an app's, phone's, or even laptop's success with the press of a button. We have an astounding amount of control over the market, and once we begin developing the same products that we enjoy, we can effectively improve the overall industry.

But in order to do that, we need to be encouraging more females to enter STEM. Right now, we're not even graduating enough engineers and computer scientists, period. There are thousands and thousands of jobs unfilled due to a lack of supply. If we enrolled the same amount of girls in STEM courses as boys, we might actually come close to meeting the demand, ultimately bettering employment rates and the economy.

So, what does the ideal future look like? Well, it'd break down into a few parts:

- Gender stereotypes are minimal to nonexistent
- Education is accessible to all citizens of the world
- STEM education is stressed and available for all those who choose to pursue it

There will be no such day where gender bias is immediately eradicated. It will be a slow process, but the past is the best indicator of the future. As the years have gone by, it's accurate to say that we've gotten more progressive as a society. Now, if the trend follows, we could be seeing major changes in small, incremental ways. It might start with the media releasing more movies and TV shows that depict strong female role models. It might start with parents showing their sons and daughters children's shows where there are strong male and female leads, both independent from each other. It might start with people adopting more progressive views, and the sexism and misogyny of the past slowly withers away. As a result, nothing will stop young girls from pursuing their dreams. On the other hand, nothing will stop young boys from pursuing their dreams either.

The perfect world will be a perfect balance of equality and a perfect display of feminism, where no side reaps more than the other, and each side views the other as equal and capable.

When children enter school, they'll be no indication of associating words with genders. When children are five, they won't immediately associate leadership and smarts with men. They'll view it as gender-neutral and hopefully will be able to see themselves in that same light one day. As they enter their general education classes, there won't be any mentalities present that group subjects by gender: no student or teacher will believe that "math and science is for boys" and "reading is for girls". Instead, everything will be accessible to everyone, and every child will have their own chance to succeed. Every child will learn what they wish to learn, with no underlying expectations of them.

We would live in a world where everyone has an equal chance to succeed. The American Dream was the first phenomenon in which it was believed that anyone, with hard work, could chase opportunity and fulfill their aspirations. However, as the years went by, it became clear that that promise was only afforded to a few. For the vast majority of people of color and women, their struggles were often amplified by the systemic discrimination they faced. In the early days, the ones who thrived were disproportionately male and overwhelmingly white. The days of Jim Crow and anti-female suffrage are over, but the beliefs of the past are far from gone.

The bias that surrounds women and people of color still rears its head, and although progress has been made, it would be inaccurate to say that we're in a "post-racial" or "post-misogynistic" world.

The first systemic change we would see is quality, free education for all. That's right: for all. Not just in the United States, Canada, or United Kingdom, but everywhere. In Pakistan, India, Myanmar, Somalia, Uganda, Nigeria, Afghanistan — not a single girl would have to sacrifice their future for the sake of their male siblings. Instead, every child, male or female, would have a chance to escape the cycle of poverty.

But this process would most likely begin at home, here, in the United States. America and other first-world countries (defined by Merriam-Webster as "the highly developed industrialized nations often considered the westernized countries of the world") would strive to improve their quality of education. Although these nations will boast a high standard of schooling, there are specific regions and areas within each country that are in serious need of money, resources, and skilled teachers. In addition to this, each nation would strive to improve their STEM education; specifically, engineering and computer science.

As more and more jobs are set to be automated in twenty years, it's imperative that we graduate students that are adequately prepared for the throes of the real world. This could be as simple as ten minutes of extra science education each class period, or offering after-school STEM activities to interested children. It could also go as far as offering advanced laboratory courses at eligible high schools, and hosting research opportunities for aspiring scientists. We're not graduating even a fraction of the engineers we need, and sooner or later, it will negatively impact our economy and technological promise. But we can't force anyone to choose a particular career path – that's something each person decides for his or her self. What we can do, however, is motivate children at a young age to pick up STEM-related activities and hobbies. It's been shown that an interest in science can be contagious and influence other, perhaps uninterested, children.

Then, we'd start seeing international organizations play a bigger role in this process. Many countries like Pakistan and Myanmar must take quick action to reverse their policies on general education, and they must take a stronger stance on equal education for all. In fact, it's absolutely imperative that partisanship and corrupt politics do not interfere with this process. Organizations like the United Nations should be actively managing the educational crisis in these countries, while the same countries make an effort to effectively cooperate and resolve the issue. The UN must push three key ideas: better quality of general education, gender equality, and free tuition.

We must be focusing on improving the standard of schooling, especially in rural areas, of these nations. In many areas, education is not regarded as a priority, while labor is. There must be laws instituted that require children to attend school to at least secondary school. Even global superpowers like India do not have laws introduced that enforce similar measures. Doing so will ensure that every world citizen has basic literacy, mathematical skills, and analytic reasoning.

We must also seek to enforce gender equality. Restricting young girls from educations cannot be tolerated anymore. Education must be regarded as a human right, as it's one of the most important gifts anyone can receive in this world. Education protects you from being taken advantage of or unjustly manipulated. It ensures that everyone can adequately understand their current situation and their place in this world. Without formal education, your life can seem as if it's in a bubble and there's no way to escape it. Therefore, girls and boys must receive the same quality of education, and either party must not be given special treatment or favor.

But, this is easier said than done. In many countries, tuition is incredibly expensive, and it's impossible for poorer families to send all their children off to school. As a result, their sons are prioritized and, as in the case in Myanmar, the girls are forced to work to pay for their brother's education. Due to cases like these, we can't expect change right away. However, the UN and similar organizations must also focus on the idea of free schooling. It will take a while, especially to allocate necessary funds and change entire school systems. But if it's done, we could be seeing a new world, inundated with promise and innovation.

Our ideal society would comprise the late Anita Borg's dream: an equal representation of 50% women in STEM industries. From a young age, girls are given a safe environment to pursue STEM interests. What does that mean? Well, it starts off with zero to minimal bias against women in tech. There won't be any beliefs in the first place claiming that science is a "boys' club" in any child's mind. Therefore, when a girl attempts to pursue STEM activities in a school or afterschool program, they'll be surrounded by many of their peers: peers of their gender, race, and ethnicity. As a result of this safe environment, many more girls will choose to stick with STEM subjects, rather than losing interest in them entirely. More and more women will matriculate into engineering and computer science related courses in college, and eventually we'll see a flood of women scientists.

But the beauty of it all will be, to the youth of that age, that it's a relatively normal thing. It won't be abnormal to your local male college student that his computer science course is half women. It won't be abnormal to your local female college student that her engineering course is half male. It will be regarded as entirely ordinary, and that's the true goal. The toxic bro-culture in tech will have disappeared and in its place an inclusive environment of collaboration and innovation is born. Around the world, in countries like the United Kingdom,

Australia, and America, we'd see significant, positive impacts on our technological advancements. Diversity would truly shape our world for the better.

But words must turn into actions, and actions must turn into progress. It's not enough anymore to say how much we care — we've got to show our efforts as well. We're only worth as much as we do. If we say that we care about the gender gap and about motivating more women to STEM, we have to keep making tangible progress to that. This ideal society is unlikely to emerge tomorrow, but that doesn't mean we can't start cultivating it today. If we start now, together, we could be making a truly significant mark on our world. They say that every generation has a few causes they fight passionately for. Let this be ours. As George Washington Carver once said, "Education is the key to unlock the golden door of freedom."

So, what have we discovered together?

Well, we've analyzed the imminent need to close the gender gap in technology. There's a simple, short, yet telling equation to exactly why:

Gender and Racial Diversity = Varied Perspectives =
More Innovation = Better Future

Diversity is absolutely crucial in making sure we're crafting a world for all of us, not just for a specific type of people. When we have engineers of all different races, ethnicities, religions, and beliefs, as well as an equal amount of men and women developers, we will see a technological world just as diverse as our Earth. And this equality is, in general, incredibly beneficial to the STEM realm as well as the consumer market. We've seen how women overall tend to positively influence their workplaces when assuming leadership positions. They generally adopt more of a democracy, ensuring that every person has an equal voice on every issue that is important to them. This is apparent in fields other than tech — it takes place in our government as well. Young white girls, Asian boys, Hispanic girls, and African-American boys all have (at least slightly) different life experiences. Their upbringings, as well as their own beliefs, have shaped who they are today. This richness in thought is what has the potential to revolutionize the way we build tech. Varied perspectives equals more innovation, which equals better fruits of our labor, and a better future.

But what exactly do we mean when we say "better future"? What's the tangible evidence of that? Well, one particular example comes to mind. Recently, a 30-year old woman made headlines for not being able to find a prosthetic leg in her skin color. Originally from Kenya, the woman had lost the lower part of her leg due to an amputation. When she was given options for a new prosthetic leg, she realized there were, in fact, only two: very light, and very dark. That's it! What this reminds me of are incidents in my elementary school classes, where we'd be assigned figures to color and draw. Whenever I'd reach for the Crayola crayons, I realized that there was only one color named "skin color". It just happened to be a tan white.

The significance of this event transcends the lack of 'skin-tone choice' for prosthesis patients. It represents a fact that many in this world are now accustomed to: not being included or feeling outside the norm. There are thousands upon thousands of skin colors and tones. Yet, there were only two to choose from. What might that say about the team who built them, or their respective biases and beliefs? I'm almost positive that if that team was comprised of people of different ethnic backgrounds, there would have been a myriad of tones for this woman to choose from. Why? Because they would personally understand the need for it.

All in all, diversity results in a better society, as a whole. Innovation is what we desperately need, and with it, we could go on to build bigger and better things quicker than we could have anticipated. This includes developments in the fields of aeronautics, apps, software, and artificial intelligence. The possibilities are, quite literally, limitless.

So, what are the solutions we have to closing the gender gap in tech? Well, we have the 3 C's to implement. If you recall, they're comprised of Change, Cooperation, and Commemoration.

In short, we must Change our biases about girls, boys, and their respective gender roles. We can do this through changing female representation in the media, and by teaching our children to adopt more inclusive views of others.

We must also Cooperate with our families, schools, and communities to broaden young girls' exposure to STEM and the sciences. By starting community science fairs, increasing the amount of STEM related activities in schools, and promoting gender-inclusive STEM campaigns, we can easily Cooperate with fellow allies to make a difference.

Lastly, we must make an active effort to Commemorate past and present women in technology and acknowledge their struggles in climbing the tech ladder.

The first step to resolving a problem is to acknowledge it — not deny it. By checking each of our privileges, we're one step closer to solving the real issues. Those who do happen to be more privileged than others shouldn't feel 'guilty' for it and counter its existence. Instead, they should be focused on making sure everyone has the same opportunities as them. This doesn't have to be the result of grand gestures — it can be as small as calling out implicit bias in the workplace, or perhaps making an active effort to employ a diverse set of workers. It can simply be regarded as doing the right thing.

But, one could say, women have been trying to change the system for years now. From the suffragette movements of the 1920's, to the gender-inclusive tech revolution of the '70s, to finally the Girls Who Code, the Lean Ins, and Malala Funds of today. What makes this particular generation of girls different? Why won't our movement be in vain? What's the point of trying when we've made little progress so far?

It's certainly a difficult set of uncertainties to tackle. No one has all the answers, but I do happen to know this: progress is not attained in a snap of the finger. Instead, it's grown over time, little by little: citizen to citizen, phrase to phrase, belief to belief. It's cultivated, fostered, and released into the wilds of society. From there, it manifests, for good, or for worse. The only thing that one is directly in control of is the action of making a change. Because without that one action, there is no chance of success. Failure is an essential part of progress, but in time, so is victory. They are two sides of the same coin and eventually you'll come across both.

We grew up in the internet age. We can't remember a time when the world wasn't available to us with the click of a switch. We consider fingerprint scanners on our phones and voice-recognition on our TVs to be completely normal. We can learn a language or raise thousands of dollars for charity on a phone app. Any piece of knowledge that was ever known to humankind is available with a quick Google search. This world was unthinkable fifty years ago. A hundred years ago, this would've been some sort of unattainable utopia. In fact, they say that the average American today lives better than the life of a king centuries past. A thousand years ago, our world would seem like a realm of the gods. But to us, it's what we've always known.

And instead of wasting that opportunity, we need to be taking full advantage of it. We're a passionate, driven generation: let's funnel all that excitement and energy into causes we believe in, into revolutions we're inspired by, and into fighting injustice and tyranny all over the globe. Sound dramatic? That's the point. We're surrounded by so much power — let's use it to change the world.

We have hope. Hope for the future, and most importantly, hope in ourselves. We believe in ourselves, and we're ready to take up arms for one another. We've fostered a new type of courage that's come from the turn of the century, and we're more than ready to face this problem head on. We're not the shy, obedient stereotypes of girls before — we're passionate activists with a cause, and we won't stop till we've made changes for the greater good. Unlike others before, we have a desire to set our own precedents: to do something that has never been done before. Let's be the ones that finally put an end to gender bias, from the start of now to however long it takes.

So, to all the girls who want to make a change, let's promise to do a couple things.

Let's promise to always persevere. To persevere through the biases, discrimination, and lack of peers. You'll get through it.

Let's promise to always pursue knowledge. To capture our own imaginations, to be a hungry, curious thinker with an insatiable appetite for learning.

Let's promise to be persistent in our cause. It won't always be easy pursuing STEM in a critical environment, but persistence is key.

Be a role model. Be a leader.

And eventually, good things will come.

RESOURCES

There's many things you can do to make a difference: get involved with your community, call out implicit bias, and stand up against sexism and misogyny. Young, old, student, parent, teacher – it doesn't matter. What matters is how we come together, cooperate, and learn from each other to cultivate a healthier, more accepting world. Here's a couple ways you, specifically, can tackle the issue of girls in STEM:

- Get Coding!
    - o Learning to code, progressing your own technological education, and gaining useful knowledge is necessary in fighting implicit bias in tech. Start coding to motivate your friends, peers, and fellow classmates to do so as well.

- o Here are some programs I've found especially useful in learning how to code online:
  - Codeacademy
    - Codeacademy is a website dedicated to teaching anyone, anywhere how to code. Their free tutorials include programming languages such as Python, JavaScript, and Ruby. Codeacademy also offers a few more less known languages, such as React and SQL. They can be accessed on www.codeacademy.org.
  - Code.org
    - Code.org is an nonprofit organization passionate about making code accessible around the globe. 20% of U.S. students have accounts on the website, and 9,000,000 of their user base is female. Code.org has worked with various governments and state legislatures to implement computer science friendly curriculum in schools. In

addition to this, they have pioneered the Hour of Code program. According to the organization, this is a "one-hour introduction to computer science, designed to demystify "code", to show that anybody can learn the basics, and to broaden participation in the field of computer science". They can be accessed at www.code.org.

- Khan Academy
  - Khan Academy is a fantastic resource for accessing any type of curriculum at any level or difficulty. In addition to their mathematics, history, science, and English courses, Khan Academy has also added computer science courses to their catalogue. Their tutorials teach basic coding, including JavaScript, HTML/CSS, and SQL. They can be accessed at www.khanacademy.org.

- MIT OpenCourseware
  - MIT OpenCourseware is an initiative pioneered by the Massachusetts Institute of Technology in making college curriculum available to anyone. Their courses cover anything from introductory to complex physics, abstract mathematics, and namely, computer science. Concepts taught may be a bit advanced from the get-go, so try starting with another program, and if curious delve into their catalogue. They can be accessed at https://ocw.mit.edu/index.htm.
- Coursera and edX
  - Coursera and edX are companies dedicated to democratizing college-level courses internationally. With curriculum from major universities, millions of users visit the website to pick up useful skills and knowledge. Coursera and edX even offers

online, accredited degrees from universities. Coursera can be accessed at https://www.coursera.org/, and edX can be accessed at https://www.edx.org/.

- Get Inspired!
  - A great way to learn what people in the industry are discussing is through TEDTalks. TEDTalks (TED standing for technology, engineering, and design) are short speeches given at TED-specific events. Anyone can speak at a TED event as long as they have an idea to share with the world – and you can even organize one in your own community. Here are a few TED talks relating to feminism, women in STEM, and code.
    - Reshma Saujani's "Teach Girls Bravery, Not Perfection:
      - https://www.ted.com/talks/reshma_saujani_teach_girls_bravery_not_perfection

- Mitch Resnick's "Let's Teach Kids How to Code"
  - https://www.ted.com/talks/mitch_resnick_let_s_teach_kids_to_code
- Ziauddin Yousafzai's "My Daughter, Malala"
  - https://www.ted.com/talks/ziauddin_yousafzai_my_daughter_malala

- Get Reading!
  - Often when tackling a cause as large as this, it's imperative to heed the advice of previous generations, all while learning from past mistakes and pressing on. Here are some of my favorite titles relating to feminism, education, and science:
    - *Lean In: Women, Work, and the Will to Lead* by Sheryl Sandberg
    - *We Should All Be Feminists* by Chimamanda Ngozi Adichie
    - *I Am Malala: How One Girl Stood Up for Education and Changed the World* by Malala Yousafzai

- Get Working!
  - There's a huge community outside of your own deeply passionate about this issue. Here's a few ways you could make a difference yourself (although the sky's the limit!):
    - Start a Girls Who Code or related organization in your hometown.
    - Lead a fundraiser to raise money for universal education, and donate the proceeds.
    - Encourage your friends to join you in a fun, coding journey.
    - Discuss the effects of gender biases with family and peers.
    - Have educated conversations with others on the importance of diversity in tech.
    - Be aware of implicit or explicit bias – and don't be afraid to call it out if you see it.

- Connect and Share
  - If you ever need any advice, help, or direction, please feel free to contact one of my two projects:

- She Dreams in Code
  - She Dreams in Code, Inc. is a recognized nonprofit dedicated to serving the Southern California area. SDIC looks to provide struggling yet promising STEM programs with the resources they need to succeed. Contact us at www.shedreamsincode.org.
- A Girl in Tech
  - A Girl in Tech, my personal project, mainly tackles the gender gap head-on by providing commentary on tech diversity and bias. Find it at www.natasharavinand.com.

ACKNOWLEDGEMENTS AND PUBLICATIONS FEATURED

This work could not have been possible without the following people and publications:

Tiffany Pham, CEO/Founder, Mogul Inc.

David Pham, CTO/CPO, Mogul Inc.

Sara Mauskopf, CEO, Winnie Inc.

Diane Barram Westgate, Senior Product Manager, Google Inc.

Shenaz Zack Mistry, Senior Product Manager, Google Inc.

Vanessa Ganaden, Senior Project Manager, Novuum Inc.

William Taormina, Founder, National Startup League

Greg Kaplan, Founder, College Path

Marina Alburger, Teacher, Northwood High School

Angie Olivares, Teacher, Northwood High School

Isabelle Zhao, undergraduate Computer Science & Economics,
Stanford University

Beede, David, Tiffany Julian, David Langdon, George McKittrick, Beethika Khan, and Mark Doms. *Women in STEM: A Gender Gap to Innovation*. Issue brief no. #04-11. Economics and Statistics Administration. U.S. Department of Commerce, Aug. 2011. Web.

Bian, Lin, Sarah-Jane Leslie, and Andrei Cimpian. "Gender Stereotypes about Intellectual Ability Emerge Early and Influence Children's Interests." *Science*. American Association for the Advancement of Science, 27 Jan. 2017. Web.

"Diversity in High Tech." *Diversity in High Tech*. U.S. Equal Employment Opportunity Commission, n.d. Web.

Eagly, Alice Hendrickson, and Linda L. Carli. *Through the Labyrinth: The Truth about How Women Become Leaders*. N.p.: Harvard Business School, 2008. Print.

"Economics & Statistics Administration." *STEM: Good Jobs Now and For the Future | Economics & Statistics Administration*. United States Department of Commerce, 14 July 2011. Web.

Education in Pakistan. Rep. Education For All Global Monitoring. N.p., Oct. 2012. Web.

"European Girls in STEM." *Empowering Government*. Microsoft, 10 May 2017. Web.

Girls' Education – the Facts. Issue brief. Education for All Global Monitoring. UNESCO, Oct. 2013. Web.

Hispanics and STEM Education. Publication. U.S. Department of Education. Department of Education, n.d. Web.

Hyde, Janet S., Sara M. Lindberg, Marcia C. Linn, Amy B. Ellis, and Caroline C. Williams. "Gender Similarities Characterize Math Performance." *Education Forum*. American Association for the Advancement of Science, 25 July 2008. Web.

Krogstad, Jens Manuel. "Key Facts about How the U.S. Hispanic Population Is Changing." *Pew Research Center*. N.p., 08 Sept. 2016. Web.

Landivar, Liana Christin. *Disparities in STEM Employment by Sex, Race, and Hispanic Origin*. Publication no. ACS-24. U.S. Census Bureau. American Community Survey Reports, Sept. 2013. Web.

Litow, Stanley. "A Silent Crisis: The Underrepresentation of Latinos in STEM Careers." *Education Week*. N.p., 04 May 2016. Web

Reubena, Ernesto, Paola Sapienzab, and Luigi Zingales. "How Stereotypes Impair Women's Careers in Science." *Proceedings of the National Academy of Sciences*. National Academy Sciences, 10 Mar. 2014. Web.

Sandberg, Sheryl, and Nell Scovell. *Lean In: Women, Work, and the Will to Lead*. N.p.: Alfred A. Knopf, 2017. Print.

"Somalia." *UNICEF Somalia - Education - Education in Somalia*. UNICEF, n.d. Web.

"Successful Programme Changing Girls' Minds about STEM Careers to Go Digital." *CA Technologies - EMEA*. N.p., 31 Jan. 2017. Web.

Voyer, D., and S. D. Voyer. "Gender Differences in Scholastic Achievement: A Meta-analysis." *Psychological Bulletin*. U.S. National Library of Medicine, July 2014. Web.

Wise. "Welcome to People Like Me." *People Like Me*. N.p., n.d. Web.

Women Who Choose Computer Science— What Really Matters. Google Inc., 26 May 2014. Web.

Wood, Julia. *Gendered Media: The Influence of Media on Views of Gender*. Tech. no. Article 7. Department of Communication, University of North Carolina at Chapel Hill. N.p., n.d. Web.

ABOUT THE AUTHOR

Natasha Ravinand is the founder of She Dreams in Code, a nonprofit dedicated to increasing tech opportunities for middle school girls. A global coding ambassador for the award-winning women's platform, Mogul, Natasha was selected as one of the top 50 influential high-schoolers in the world. She has extensively researched how the childhood implications of gender biases contribute to the lack of women in scientific careers. Natasha frequently writes on her personal website www.natasharavinand.com and on Twitter @natasharavinand.

CPSIA information can be obtained
at www.ICGtesting.com
Printed in the USA
BVHW031258040219
539429BV00001B/60/P